# Interviews & Assessments

*The **Insider Guides** is a dynamic series of books which together form the ultimate career companion.*

*Whether looking for that first job, or hoping to develop your current career, each title in the series offers practical advice and real-life insights to put you on the inside track to success.*

Other titles in the series:

**Job Search**
Brian Sutton

**Career Networking**
Brian Sutton

# Interviews & Assessments

## Succeeding at selection and getting the job you want

by

Brian Sutton

First published in 2000 by
The Industrial Society
Robert Hyde House
48 Bryanston Square
London W1H 2EA

© Brian Sutton 2000

ISBN 1 85835 820 5

**British Library Cataloguing-in-Publication Data.
A catalogue record for this book is available from
the British Library.**

Typeset by: The Midlands Book Typesetting Company
Printed by: Cromwell Press
Cover by: Sign Design
Cover image by: Trevor Bonderud/Images

The Industrial Society is a Registered Charity No. 290003

# CONTENTS

## ACKNOWLEDGEMENTS

It is a pleasure to acknowledge the help I've received from all those who have provided me with views and opinions quoted in this book.

To my editor, Susannah Lear, I owe a special debt of gratitude for offering me the opportunity to write all three books in this important career series. Thank you also to Aine Gray, Research Consultant at SHL, for her help with the selection test examples, reproduced here with kind permission of SHL Group plc.

Last, but by no means least, I'm grateful to my wife Jacquey for her distinctive blend of encouragement and support.

# INTRODUCTION

Whatever your career or job-search plans, you'll need a good understanding of how today's job market works, combined with effective job-search and networking skills and a well thought-out strategy for dealing with interviews and other selection methods.

The first two books in this series, *Job Search* and *Career Networking*, provide all the advice and guidance you need to locate jobs and win interviews. This book, *Interviews & Assessments*, focuses on the key issues you should know when you've been invited to attend an interview or some other selection method.

Selection is a crucial aspect of any employer's operation. Consequently, many now focus their attention on improving the process to ensure that only the best candidates are appointed. Faced with increasingly sophisticated selection techniques, what can you do to improve your chances of success?

Interviewing is still the most widely used selection method. For some people it can be an unnerving experience, filling them with fear and dread. However, with proper self-assessment, a good understanding of your transferable skills, personal strengths, achievements, and adequate preparation, it needn't be an ordeal.

The use of psychometric tests is becoming more common, a direct result of employers' concern that the people they recruit should be a good 'fit' both for the job and their company culture. In the changing world of work, there is increased recognition of the impact of personal make-up on many jobs and a new emphasis on the need to take account of personality in building and maintaining teams.

An important theme running through this series is the need for good preparation. In this case, what you do *before* an interview determines what you do in the interview. Approaching an interview, or any other selection method for that matter, without adequate preparation is to risk encountering continual rejection.

Whether you're looking for your first job or planning your next career move, returning to work after bringing up a family or facing redundancy, this book will help you to market yourself correctly during interviews and face up to other selection methods with confidence

**so that you CAN succeed in winning that job!**

Part One focuses on achieving interview success. The first chapter describes the interview methods used by different interviewers, while Chapter 2 advises how best to deal with these different interview styles and questioning techniques adopted by today's employers.

The importance of interview preparation is highlighted in Chapter 3, with examples of the ten most common interview questions.

Body language accounts for 70% of what we communicate. Chapter 4 explains how taking care of your appearance and mastering your body language can favourably influence the interviewer.

Chapter 5 offers really good advice on how to conduct yourself immediately before and during the interview.

Chapter 6 contains advice on how to handle both success and rejection.

Part Two deals with other selection methods. Chapter 7 examines psychometric tests and the role they play in the selection process, while Chapter 8 describes the increasing use of assessment centres in recruitment and the most common types of exercises.

A few UK employers use handwriting analysis while an even smaller number employ astronomy and psychic analysis as a selection method. Whilst, thankfully, such methods remain on the fringe, Chapter 9 completes the picture on selection methods.

The final chapter summarises the key points of success at interview and selection.

With checklists, case studies, quotes from employers and recruitment specialists, plus myth busters that challenge commonly held beliefs, *Interviews & Assessments* should provide all the practical help and support you need. Read in conjunction with the other two books in this series, you will have the complete guide to career and job-search success.

# part one  interview success

## INTERVIEWS WITH EMPLOYERS

Whilst interviewing is an imperfect selection tool, it remains the most widely used method for selecting employees, enabling employers to evaluate candidates' experience, skills, personal strengths and achievements. It has been described as a mutual exchange of information because it also provides candidates with an opportunity to gain information about the organisation and the post for which they have applied, and to evaluate how these match their own skills, personal strengths and career goals. An interview is an exchange of information that will enable both employer and candidate to make a decision.

In an attempt to improve the predictive validity of interviewing, many employers have introduced a variety of interview procedures. Here are some examples of the methods you're likely to come across:

- exploratory interviews
- one-to-one interviews
- shortlist interviews
- sequential interviews
- panel interviews and selection boards
- group interviews
- telephone interviews
- virtual interviews
- social interviews.

### Exploratory interviews

This type of interview might be conducted by a line manager or personnel officer at an 'open day' or career fair held away from company premises in informal surroundings. This informal approach is often used as a way of promoting the employer and enabling candidates to find out more about the available vacancies.

## One-to-one interviews

This is the most familiar method of selection. It involves face-to-face discussion, provides the best opportunity to exchange information and enables you to establish rapport with the interviewer, who is usually a line manager. The line manager usually has the authority to make the offer of employment, although they may still need to brief their senior manager about the chosen candidate.

## Shortlist interviews

It is common for suitable candidates to be invited back for a second interview to meet a more senior person who has some say in the selection decision. Whilst some of the questions you were previously asked about your skills and experience may be repeated, it's more likely that the second interviewer will try to determine whether you'd be a good fit for that department and the organisation.

## Sequential interviews

In the sequential interview the first interview, conducted by either a personnel officer or junior manager, is followed by a second interview with a different line manager and possibly a personnel officer. Interviewers don't often meet in advance to prepare their area of questioning, so expect to be asked the same questions at both interviews.

'If you have an interview with several people at a particular company on the same day, don't make the mistake of thinking the second interviewer knows which questions you were asked during the first interview. I've even known candidates to say "I was asked that question earlier on today." Keep yourself fresh for every new interview and be prepared to repeat the story of your career.'

*Personnel director – publishing industry*

## Panel interviews and selection boards

In panel interviews, the candidate will usually meet with two or three interviewers, typically a personnel manager and several line managers, whilst a selection board can involve up to eight interviewers. Both panel interviews and selection boards are formal in tone and you're most likely to come across them for public sector and academic jobs, and occasionally for senior jobs in industry and commerce.

Most people find panel interviews and selection boards intimidating and stressful. The most difficult aspect, particularly with selection boards, is coping with the various interviewers' different personalities and styles of communication. Some may adopt a formal approach, whilst others are more relaxed in their style of questioning. Questions are often unplanned and the more dominating members of the board, or its chairperson, can overwhelm the judgements of the others.

Faced with an invitation to either a panel interview or selection board, bear in mind that they tend to favour the more confident and articulate candidates.

'The best advice I can give to any candidate attending a panel interview is first of all to prepare well. Get to know the company and its products or services. Secondly, because this type of interview can be stressful, many candidates feel compelled to provide quick answers and often their response has not been thought through. Don't be rushed into giving quick answers; take time to consider your response.'

*Establishment officer – local government*

## Group interviews

Group interviews are used by large organisations recruiting for jobs where there is a heavy investment in training. You and five or six other candidates will be interviewed together by one or more interviewer. The group may be asked to discuss a topic rather than answer specific questions, which may involve problems or issues directly relevant to the post for which you're applying. Group interviews can often include a series of exercises and tests.

## Telephone interviews

Telephone interviews can be one of the most uncomfortable experiences of the job-search process. Employers tend to use this method when they've had a large response to an advertisement and need to disqualify unlikely candidates. It's precisely because employers are looking for reasons to disqualify rather than select that candidates feel so uncomfortable.

It's much harder to establish rapport with the interviewer on the phone. They can make judgements not so much on what you say but the way you say it. There is also the problem of unfilled silence-space when you're unsure who should speak next. This rarely happens in one-to-one interviews because eye contact and other body language act as visual signals to who-does-what-next.

'If you receive a call out of the blue requesting further information in response to an application for employment, tell the caller that it's a little inconvenient at the moment and could they phone you again in 15 minutes. This will give you an opportunity to find the original advertisement and put together a few thoughts about how best to sell yourself during the telephone interview.'

*Recruitment manager – gas services*

## Virtual interviews

If you find yourself sitting in front of a video camera answering questions, you're taking part in a virtual interview. The interviewer may be in the room with you but is also just as likely to be remote from you in another room, from where they will communicate with you via a microphone and loudspeaker. Your responses to the questions will be observed on a video screen. At the conclusion of the exercise, a panel of people assesses the recorded interviews and selects the best candidates to attend a face-to-face interview. Organisations that use this technique claim that it's an effective tool for the preliminary stages of selection and helps to rule out subjectivity.

From the candidate's viewpoint, talking directly to a screen means they can't build a relationship with the interviewer. Because the whole process is rather cold and distant, you're less likely to give your best performance.

'If you're offered a virtual interview, you should practise your presentation skills. Some candidates, particularly those who are easily spooked by talking into a video camera, find it very hard, because they have a strong need to establish rapport with the interviewer.'

*Client manager – recruitment consultants*

### Social interviews

Social interviews can take place over breakfast, lunch or dinner and are usually arranged at the request of a very busy employer. As with any other type of interview, all the normal rules apply, but make sure you know your table manners! Aim to select something from the menu that's easy to eat, and for obvious reasons avoid foods such as spaghetti or noodles. Even if your interviewer is consuming alcohol and offers you a drink, politely decline and ask for a soft drink. Be warned! Alcohol may just dampen your senses enough to affect your speech and what you say.

## INTERVIEWS WITH HEADHUNTERS

### The phone call

When a headhunter contacts you by phone, it means that their research may have identified you as a person with the experience, skills and personal qualities for a job with one of their clients. Before you respond to the headhunter, think carefully about whether you can speak freely and if you might need some time to gather your thoughts. If you're unsure about what to do next, ask the headhunter if you can call back later in the day, or ask them to ring you at home when there's less chance of your conversation being interrupted.

When you next speak to the headhunter, they should make it clear whether you've been approached as a possible candidate or as a source of information about other people who might be interested in the job. They won't disclose the name of their client until you've met face to face and they're satisfied that you meet all the client's requirements. However, you should be given the following information:

- A description of the job and what experience and qualifications are required.
- The level of the job and the title of the job to which it reports.
- Why the organisation is recruiting.
- The market in which the organisation operates and whether it's a new or well-established organisation.
- Brief details of the organisation's turnover, etc.

Salary is not usually included in this list. This is because companies who use headhunters are often prepared, within reason, to pay what it takes to obtain the right candidate. When salary is mentioned, it's often a sign that there's very little room for negotiation because pay will have been fixed by the client. Salary information is also provided to eliminate those whose earnings are already too close to this figure. If you're not interested in the job, make this clear to the headhunter, but emphasise that you'd like to maintain contact in case they handle something more appropriate in the future.

## The interview

If you're selected for interview, it means that you've already been shortlisted. Expect a lengthy interview – some take more than two hours – and the possibility that psychometric testing may be included. The interview will focus more on your knowledge of the industry and the personal chemistry between the candidate and client rather than transferable skills and past achievements. Finally, you can expect to be interviewed by the client. At this point, you should know a great deal more about the job and the organisation. If you have any concerns, it's best to resolve them now before proceeding to the final interview.

**MYTH BUSTER**

*Headhunters are only interested in interviewing candidates who are already in employment*

Not true! In today's job market, there are many excellent candidates who have lost their jobs because of organisational change. Headhunters are fully aware of this and welcome the opportunity to interview these candidates.

## INTERVIEWS WITH RECRUITMENT CONSULTANTS

Recruitment consultants usually advertise on behalf of their client and often do so without disclosing their name. If you've responded to an advertisement and have been selected for interview, you can expect to be told the name of the client during the interview. However, because you've been given this information so late it won't help you to prepare for the interview.

Typically, an interview with a recruitment consultant will last over an hour. Often it will begin with the consultant describing the client and the job, during which time you'll be invited to ask questions. The consultant will then ask questions to establish whether your background, skills, achievements and personal qualities are a good match for the client's requirements. Your career objectives and salary needs will be discussed to determine whether the client company is in a position to meet them. The consultant will then close the interview with a brief outline of the next stage in the selection process and the likely timescale.

Interviews with headhunters and recruitment consultants are normally held in informal surroundings, usually a hotel with rooms furnished specifically for the purpose. Don't be taken in too much by this informality;

keep your wits about you at all times. The interviewer will be interested in your views about a range of subjects touching on the job, such as management style, teamwork and motivation, etc. They'll also be assessing whether your chemistry will be a good fit with their client.

## INTERVIEWS WITH EMPLOYMENT AGENCIES

Employment agencies work by sending candidates to employers who've registered their vacancies. If you're successful, the agency receives a commission from their client. You need to shop around to find the best agency for you, because they vary in the type and level of vacancy they handle. If you've already registered with an agency, they may contact you when a suitable vacancy occurs, or more likely, advertise their vacancies in the local newspaper.

If you see a job advertised that might be of interest, it's a good idea to phone the agency first to check that it's still available, to get some more information about the post and to make an appointment. Some agencies may wish to pre-screen applicants on the phone. If this happens to you, make sure that you're clear about the duties and job requirements, so that you can present your experience and skills in the best possible light.

When you first arrive at the agency, they will ask you to complete one of their standard forms. Be sure to take a copy of your CV with you to attach to the form, and use it as a guide for its completion. For some jobs, typically secretarial, you may be asked to take a skill test of your typing speed, shorthand or operation of a VDU.

Treat any interview with employment agency staff seriously. First impressions are important, so make sure your appearance and presentation are good. Try to build up a rapport, since you want to be remembered as much for your personal skills as for your experience and achievements. If the agency is satisfied that you're a good match for the vacancy, they'll phone their client with a thumbnail sketch of your background and experience and arrange an appointment. If you've registered with the agency but there are no suitable vacancies at present, keep in touch with the person who conducted your interview.

---

# REMEMBER

✔ Exploratory interviews are an informal way of promoting the employer and enabling candidates to find out more about the available vacancies.

✔ One-to-one interviews provide the best opportunity to exchange information and establish rapport with the interviewer.

✔ Panel interviews and selection boards are typically formal in tone. You're most likely to come across them for public sector and academic jobs and occasionally for senior jobs in industry and commerce.

✔ Group interviews comprise five or six other candidates who'll be interviewed together by one or more interviewer. A selection test may be included.

✔ Employers use telephone interviews when they've had a large response to an advertisement and need a method of disqualifying unlikely candidates.

✔ With virtual interviews, you'll find yourself sitting in front of a video camera answering questions.

✔ Social interviews can take place over breakfast, lunch or dinner, usually at the request of a very busy employer.

✔ If a headhunter selects you for interview, you can expect it to last two or more hours and include psychometric tests.

✔ Recruitment consultants usually advertise on behalf of their client. If you're selected for interview, don't be taken in by the informality; keep your wits about you at all times.

✔ Treat any interview with employment agency staff seriously. Give a good account of yourself and try to build up a rapport.

## INTERVIEW STANDARDS

Good interviewers know what they're looking for and how to set about finding it, largely because they are trained and have practised their skills. They are thorough in their preparation and take a completely structured approach using well thought-out questions. Poor interviewers fail to prepare, ask inappropriate questions and select on the basis of hunch, instinct or gut feeling. Expect to come across interviewers of all types. Some will talk too much, leaving you little opportunity to sell yourself, whilst others will hardly talk at all, expecting you to fill the space without any real guidance. Some interviewers take control of the interview process, whilst others employ a laid-back interview style. Be prepared for any situation, adequately prepare beforehand, keep a cool head, and treat every interview as a learning opportunity.

> 'Some careers books by American authors suggest that you should take control of the interview. I can't speak for American employers, but here in the UK, this wouldn't work. Employers hold the cards, because they're the ones with the jobs; this doesn't mean you shouldn't find or indeed make opportunities to demonstrate your skills and strengths, but adopting a style which is both forward and pushy won't endear you to most interviewers.'
>
> *Sales director – office equipment suppliers*

## STRUCTURED INTERVIEWS

Structured interviews follow a logical progression where each candidate is asked the same predetermined questions and their responses are compared both against each other and against the requirements of the job. The interviewer is likely to be a personnel officer or a line manager who has received interview training. A description of the job and the ideal candidate would have been prepared to help the interviewer, who will then ask questions that probe the key areas.

Structured interviews normally operate along the following lines:

- The interview will begin with some small-talk to put you at ease.
- This will be followed by a description of the interview format and what's expected of you.
- The interviewer will describe the job you've applied for, along with some brief information about the organisation.
- Next, the interviewer will ask questions prompted by the content of your CV. This will include your education and recent work history.
- The interviewer will then move on to questions about your skills, strengths, weaknesses and achievements.
- You may be asked about your interests and hobbies.
- You'll be invited to ask questions of your own.
- The interviewer may give you some information about salary and benefits, or this may be deferred to a shortlist interview.
- The interviewer will close the interview by giving you some information about the next steps in the process: when you can expect to hear the outcome of your interview, if there's to be a second interview, etc.

Some employers use a competency approach to structured interviews. Competence in its broadest sense refers to the clusters of related knowledge, skills, abilities, personal strengths and motivations that individuals apply to the successful achievement of a job. To identify what those clusters of knowledge and skills are, employers study high-performing occupants of the same job. What emerges is a blueprint of the skills and personal strengths that make a difference between outstanding and average performance. These findings are then included in the person specification and systematically applied to the assessment of candidates applying for the same job.

## BEHAVIOURAL INTERVIEWS

The interview will probably begin like any other, with the usual exchange of pleasantries, but then the interviewer will ask you an unusual or specific question. For example: 'What was the most stressful situation you've ever experienced, and how did you go about handling it?' This type of question is designed to elicit information about your actual behaviour in a variety of real work or social situations and hypothetical circumstances.

In a more traditional interview, a typical question might be 'How would you deal with an irate customer?' You can probably guess that the interviewer would like you to say 'I'd be sympathetic and ask them to tell me about their problem, then I'd offer my assistance in resolving the problem.' This appears to be quite a good answer, but the problem is that it's theoretical. It doesn't represent what you'd actually do in that situation. In a behavioural interview, the same question would be rephrased as follows: 'Give me a specific example of an occasion when you had to deal with an irate customer. What was the problem and what was the outcome?'

Many of the questions in behavioural interviews are deliberately negative: for example, 'Tell me about an occasion when an error of yours cost your employer time and money.' You'll probably try and come up with an answer that doesn't show you in a bad light. The interviewer immediately responds with 'Is that the worst error you've ever made?' Negative questions are very difficult to answer and if you try to dodge the real issue, the interviewer has been trained to press even harder to get to the truth.

The whole idea behind behavioural interviews is that

your past is the best predictor of the future. Consequently, you must give answers that demonstrate your skills, experience and personal strengths rather than answers that deal with generalities.

If you're not well prepared for behavioural interviews, they can be disastrous. All the help and support you need is provided in the next chapter.

## MYTH BUSTER

### *There's nothing to learn from attending behavioural interviews if all the questions are hypothetical*

*Not true! There's often more than a little truth hidden somewhere in these questions, and you can learn quite a lot about the company, its objectives and its problems. Interviewers are not only looking for answers that demonstrate experience and achievements, they're also looking for evidence of your resourcefulness and skills of innovation and creativity.*

## CONVERSATIONAL INTERVIEWS

In a conversational interview, you may be lulled into thinking you're talking to a friend rather than a prospective employer. The style is as far removed from structured and behavioural interviews as you can get. You'll find the interviewer very relaxed and friendly. They'll often begin the interview by telling you a great deal about the job and the organisation and will want to discuss their new products and services or any changes that may be occurring in the industry.

Conversational interviews usually comprise requests for information rather than specific questions. For example: 'What was it like to manage such a large number of people?' rather than 'What problems were there in managing such a large number of staff?'; or, 'What did you enjoy most about working for that company?' rather than 'What was your most significant contribution when working for that company?'

Conversational interviews are often conducted by unskilled, badly prepared interviewers who fail to get the best out of candidates. From the candidate's viewpoint, it is all too easy to forget that you're there to sell yourself.

> 'In conversational interviews, you can be easily fooled into thinking the interviewer is an amateur. This may not always be the case. In any event, candidates would be wise not to relax their guard. Whatever the interviewer's style, always aim to present yourself in the best possible light.'
>
> *HR manager – electrical engineering*

## STRESS INTERVIEWS

Whilst this type of interview is uncommon, some companies recruiting for well-paid but stressful sales jobs still use this technique. The purpose is to weed out applicants who clearly wouldn't be able to cope with the stress and pressures of the job.

In stress interviews, the interviewer may appear angry, brusque, discourteous and even somewhat disinterested. They will ask tough questions that you may find difficult to relate to the job, and you may be asked to 'sell' the benefits of an object on the table in front of you. Pressure will be applied throughout the interview, as almost everything you say will be challenged.

This type of interview isn't for the faint-hearted. To be successful you must be very confident and assertive.

> 'When you're faced with a stress interview, if you take the process personally then you're bound to come unstuck. It's best to keep in mind that it's just another style of interviewing. Think of the interviewers as acting out a role.'
>
> *Sales director – office equipment suppliers*

## QUESTIONING TECHNIQUES

Apart from specific interview styles, you can also be asked many different kinds of questions. These fall into the following categories:

### Closed questions

Closed questions elicit only a 'Yes' or 'No' response. They begin with 'Do you … ', 'Are you … ', 'Have you … ', 'Did you … ', 'Were you … ', 'Could you … ', 'Can you … ', 'Would you … ', 'Is it … ' and 'Was it … '. Here are some examples:

- *'Were you successful in your last job?'*
- *'Can you handle staff complaints?'*
- *'Were you responsible for stock control?'*
- *'Have you always exceeded your sales target?'*

Closed questions are the province of the untrained interviewer. Simply answering 'Yes' or 'No' won't help your cause. Instead, seize the opportunity to expand your answer by using illustrations. In response to the last question above, for example, you could say: *'Yes, and I've also been successful in acquiring a large amount of new business, which otherwise would have gone to our competitors.'*

### Open-ended questions

Open-ended questions can't be answered with a simple 'Yes' or 'No', but require a more lengthy and considered response. These questions always begin with 'Why … ', 'What … ', 'How … ', and 'Tell me about … '. Here are some examples:

- *'Tell me about yourself.'*
- *'Tell me about a time when you had to make a difficult decision.'*
- *'How did you go about solving that problem?'*
- *'What was the most important aspect of your work?'*
- *'Why were you asked to manage the new office?'*

## Hypothetical questions

Hypothetical questions are used to test your ability to think on your feet, and many people find them difficult to answer. Here are some examples:

- *'If you were suspicious that someone working for you was stealing company stationery, what would you do?'*
- *'Your manager has countermanded one of your orders in front of your staff. How would you deal with this?'*

Some hypothetical questions may be asked to test your integrity. For example:

- *'Whilst we have to give customers a good service and be courteous to them at all times, I often think many of them don't deserve it. Don't you agree?'*

This question is deliberately framed as a statement, with a closed question added on to deliberately provoke a 'yes' answer. Don't be tempted to answer 'yes' to avoid disagreeing with the interviewer. If you do so, they will either rule you out or ask a difficult follow-up question that will make you feel very embarrassed.

## Stress questions

Some interviewers like to include a few stress questions to test the candidate's resilience. Here are some examples:

- *'What makes you think you can do this job?'*
- *'I think you've stayed rather too long with your current employer, don't you?'*
- *'We like our staff to put in as many hours as it takes to do the job. Could you cope with this?'*
- *'With your background, we believe you're over qualified for this position. Why have you applied for this job?'*

## Probing questions

An interviewer will usually ask probing questions to get you to expand on your previous answer or simply to elicit more information. Here are some examples:

- 'Why did you find your last job so tedious?'
- 'Why do you think it's so important for a manager to be an effective problem-solver?'
- 'These are very impressive achievements. How did your company benefit from them?'

### Technical questions

Interviewers ask these questions to establish the extent of your experience in a particular field. Here are some examples:

- 'Tell me about your experience.'
- 'Describe the process you go through to complete that particular task.'
- 'What experience do you have that makes you particularly qualified for this job?'

### Multiple questions

Candidates are often confused by these questions, because they contain several different questions within one. Give yourself enough time, and answer each question in the order in which they were delivered. Here are a couple of examples:

- 'What did you enjoy doing most in your last job and what do you plan to be doing in the next five years?'
- 'What is your management style and how well do you work under pressure?'

## THE ROLE OF SILENCE

Interviewers use silence to draw out further information and to test whether your last answer was genuine. The approach involves asking a question that requires only a short answer. The format usually goes like this:

**Interviewer:**    'Are you motivated more by money than job satisfaction?'

**Candidate:**    'I think they're equally important.'

Silence.

**Candidate:**      *'I suppose, at the end of the day, it all comes down to money.'*

**Interviewer:**    *'So if we paid you enough, you'd be perfectly happy doing a routine job?'*

It's easy to see how you can make it difficult for yourself by rushing in to fill the space created by the interviewer's silence. If this happens to you, remain calm. Think carefully before answering the question and then respond as fully as possible. This will make it difficult for the interviewer to fall back on silence, but if they do use this ploy, maintain your own silence; take a quick, hopeful look at the interviewer but don't stare them out. Put pressure on the interviewer to break the silence. Here's a rerun of the previous situation using this technique:

**Interviewer:**    *'Are you motivated more by money than job satisfaction?'*

**Candidate:**      *'I'd need to be offered both in sufficient quantity before taking up a new job.'*

Silence.

**Interviewer:**    *'I see that you're currently earning £28K; if we offered you this job, what would you consider sufficient money?'*

---

### Case Study

### The nervous interviewer

Karen, a very competent office supervisor, decided that the time had come to develop her career by moving to another employer. She responded to an advert in her local paper for a job as an office manager with a small firm of accountants.

Karen was selected for interview and arrived in good time at the employer's office. The interview started 15 minutes later than scheduled. Somewhat apprehensive, Karen was introduced to John, the accountant responsible for staff management. Karen was expecting him to shake her hand and to tell her to take a seat. Instead, he sat down in his own chair and started looking for Karen's CV. This put Karen completely off her stride.

Throughout the interview, there was very little eye contact

from John. The questions he asked seemed to be aimed solely at discovering Karen's ability to get on with other people. He appeared nervous and was obviously uncomfortable with the interview process.

Karen felt very disappointed with the entire interview and wasn't surprised when, a few days later, she received a letter stating that she wouldn't be offered the job. When she evaluated her own performance at the interview, Karen realised that she'd let the situation deteriorate. Instead, she should have seized the opportunity to put the interviewer at ease whilst telling him why she was the most suitable candidate for the job.

# REMEMBER

✔ You can expect to come across interviewers of all types, so adequately prepare beforehand, keep a cool head, and treat every interview as a learning opportunity.

✔ Structured interviews follow a logical progression. Questions are asked of each candidate and their responses are compared both against each other and against the requirements of the job.

✔ Questions asked in behavioural interviews are often unusual and specific. They operate on the basis that your past is the best predictor of the future. Consequently, you must give answers that demonstrate your skills, experience and personal strengths rather than replies that address only generalities.

✔ Conversational interviews usually comprise requests for information rather than specific questions.

✔ The purpose of stress interviews is to weed out applicants who clearly wouldn't be able to cope with the stress and pressures of the job.

✔ Closed questions are ones that can extract only a 'Yes' or 'No' response. Be careful always to expand your answer.

✔ Open-ended questions can't be answered with a simple 'Yes' or 'No', but require a more lengthy and considered response.

✔ Hypothetical questions are used to test your ability to think on your feet.

✔ Stress questions test your resilience.

✔ Probing questions get you to expand on your previous answer or provide more information.

✔ Technical questions are asked to establish the extent of your experience in a particular field.

✔ Multiple questions contain several different questions within one.

✔ Interviewers use silence to draw out further information and to test whether your last answer was genuine.

## WHY PREPARATION IS IMPORTANT

Arriving at an interview unprepared is like saying to the employer 'I don't care enough about this job' or 'I can't be bothered to put in any effort'. Interviewers place a great deal of importance on preparation and will soon be able to tell whether you're bluffing your way through it. A lack of preparation can also have a detrimental effect on your self-confidence as well as increasing your anxiety level. Distinguish yourself from the rest of the candidates by thorough preparation and research, and utilise your findings effectively throughout the interview.

To prepare for interviews you need to:

- understand yourself and what you have to offer
- familiarise yourself with the position you've applied for
- familiarise yourself with the employing organisation, its products and services
- familiarise yourself with the industry you'll be working in
- prime yourself for the ten most common interview questions
- rehearse the questions you'd like to ask the interviewer
- be aware of the importance of your appearance and body language (see Chapter 4).

## UNDERSTANDING WHAT YOU HAVE TO OFFER

The first step in preparing yourself for interviews is self-assessment. If you've read the first book in this series entitled *Job Search*, you'll recall how important this is to the process of job search. Now that you're being invited to attend interviews, you need to call to mind your transferable skills, personal strengths and achievements. Focusing on these, and not on your weaknesses, will ensure that you accentuate the positive and eliminate the negative.

## Transferable skills

Transferable skills are those you acquire throughout life – at university, as you move from job to job, at home or undertaking voluntary, charitable or sporting activities.

Transferable skills can be divided into the following five families:

- people skills
- reasoning and judging skills
- co-ordinating skills
- information skills, and
- originating skills.

If you've not already done so, list your own transferable skills under each group and be sure to rank each of them so that you're clear about which skills are your strongest assets. If you need any help with this exercise, you'll find a list of transferable skills in the skills guide at the back of this book.

## Personal strengths

Recognising and understanding your personal strengths will support the transferable skills you've identified. Begin the process of identifying your personal strengths by looking for evidence of achievements at work, university or college and home. Next, list the strengths you possess that have played a role in these achievements. If you need any help with this exercise, again you'll find a list of personal strengths in the skills guide at the back of this book.

## Achievements

Achievements are tasks that you've accomplished successfully through effort, practice or perseverance, using your skills and personal strengths. To prepare your list of achievements, consider your employment history, concentrating on what is most recent. Next, refer to your list of skills and personal strengths. Think carefully about each job and pick out anything significant or of particular interest.

Understanding yourself and what you have to offer will help you to answer the interviewer's questions. You'll be able to give a much more confident account of yourself and shouldn't be caught out by interviewers asking you to reveal your weaknesses.

## FAMILIARISE YOURSELF WITH THE JOB

You should find out as much as possible about the job for which you have applied: what the duties are and what skills and qualifications are required.

When you receive a letter inviting you for interview, if the employer or recruitment consultant hasn't included a job description and employee specification, phone them and ask for copies to be sent as soon as possible. Study these documents carefully, along with the advertisement if the job was advertised in the press.

## FAMILIARISE YOURSELF WITH THE EMPLOYER

If you've applied for a job knowing who the employer is, it's well worth conducting some research. You need to know about the company's history; what sets it apart from its competitors; details of its products and services; who are its most important customers; what new developments are taking place; its sales turnover and the names of its main directors and senior managers. However, if you've applied to a recruitment consultant who placed an advertisement without revealing the employer's name, there's nothing you can do about it. If the industry was mentioned in the advertisement, then you should carry out some research at your local library.

One of the best ways to learn about an organisation is to phone their public relations department and request a copy of their annual report. You may also find that they can supply you with a pack of useful information about the company, its products and services.

Public libraries are also a good source of information about employers. Here's a list of publications that can be found in larger public libraries:

- *The Times 1000.* This is a directory of the top 1,000 largest UK companies, ranked by turnover. Contains data on size, main activity, number of employees and key personnel. Published by Times Books.
- *The Personnel Manager's Yearbook.* Lists prominent companies, with names of personnel and human resource executives and a useful directory of recruitment specialists. Published by A. P. Information Services.
- *Who Owns Whom.* A cross-referencing of interlocking holdings and affiliations. Volume one indexes parent companies followed by subsidiaries. Volume two lists subsidiaries followed by their parent company. Updated quarterly. Published by Dun and Bradstreet.
- *Confederation of Chambers of Commerce Directory.* Each directory covers the specific part of the country in which you live and lists names of member companies of all sizes, together with contact names, addresses, phone numbers and activities. Some libraries have these in their reference section.
- *Kelly's Business Directory.* Contains information on over 82,000 industrial, commercial and professional organisations in the UK. Provides names, addresses, phone numbers and a brief description. Published by Kelly's Directories.
- *Whitaker's Almanac.* Useful if you need information on employers, societies and institutions, trade associations and unions, industrial research centres, the press, banks, etc. Published by J. Whitaker and Sons Ltd.

- *Handbook of Market Leaders.* Reveals who's on top, sector by sector. Published by Extel Financial Ltd.

There will almost certainly be a trade magazine covering the industry in which you are interested. Ask your library if they have any copies and see if there's any mention of the company you're going to visit. Professional magazines published for members of a particular profession are also a useful source of company information.

You needn't limit your research to the public library. Today, information is far more accessible than ever before. The Internet is constantly evolving, and provides the most up-to-date information you're likely to find. Even smaller organisations often have a corporate website, where a lot of the information, including a profile of the company, its products and services, can often be found. Some sites provide a link to a designated recruitment page, which you may have already used to locate the job. The recruitment page often contains helpful information such as the organisation's overall strategy and its culture.

A list of useful search engines with their website addresses can be found in the resource directory at the back of this book. If you don't have the company's website address, try a 'keyword' search on one of the search engines. National newspapers including *The Times*, *Daily Telegraph* and *Observer* all have websites where you can obtain recent company information using a keyword search.

Another excellent source of information about an organisation is its employees. If you know someone who works for the company, make contact, and find out as much as you can.

## FAMILIARISE YOURSELF WITH THE INDUSTRY

You need to find out who the main players are in the industry, what size market share your prospective employer has and what challenges the industry is facing. Phone the appropriate trade organisation (refer to 'Sources of career and industry information' at the back of this book) and ask them to send you further information. You may also find trade magazines in your library with helpful articles about the industry you're researching.

> 'Not preparing well is a common trait among certain managers. They seem to think that interviewers won't call on them because they've reached a senior level. This type of thinking is dangerous, because most interviewers will assume that a manager has prepared himself for the interview.'
>
> *Recruitment consultant – management appointments*
>
> 'I like people coming to interview to have prepared. The ones who phone up and say to me, "Could you put a copy of the Annual Report in the post?" go up in my estimation several points.'
>
> *Managing director – pharmaceuticals manufacturer*

## THE TEN MOST COMMON INTERVIEW QUESTIONS

In the following pages, you'll find the ten most common interview questions, along with sample answers. Don't memorise the answers with a view to repeating them parrot fashion during the interview. Should you do so, your answers will sound false and unnatural. These examples have been provided to help you prepare for your interview, so use them to spark off your own ideas. Always listen carefully to what the interviewer says, because these questions can be worded in many different ways. With adequate preparation, you'll be able to provide effective answers to these questions and deliver them in a sincere and natural way.

### 1. 'Tell me about yourself'

It's difficult to understand why interviewers ask this question knowing that some candidates can take 30 minutes or longer to complete their answer. Despite this, it remains a very common question, and it is particularly difficult to answer, because it doesn't provide any parameters or spell out any specific requirements. Should, for example, the candidate start with where they were

born, their full-time education or first job? Does the
interviewer want information about the candidate's
personality or is the question aimed only at extracting a
summary of their experience and career progress?
Sometimes an interviewer will ask this question at the
beginning of the interview simply to relax the candidate
and get them talking. However, more often than not, it's
used to test whether you can organise, summarise and
succinctly present your experience and skills, your career
and current situation.

This question requires a great deal of preparation.
Although it may not require a lengthy reply, you still have
to decide what should be included and the order of
presentation. Furthermore, first impressions are important,
and because this is often the first question you need to get
off to a good start. Here are some guidelines to help you:

- Limit the content of your answer to any job-
  related experience, skills and achievements that are
  relevant to the job.
- Avoid including anything of a personal nature
  unless you're confident that this will be relevant and
  benefit your application.
- Be concise and stick to the facts, otherwise the
  interviewer will lose interest.
- Use an appropriate form of words to make sure
  the interviewer knows you've finished answering
  the question.
- Aim to answer the question in two minutes. A lot
  can be said in this time.
- Prepare and practise your answer and make it
  sound as natural as possible.

Carefully preparing the content so that it highlights your
strengths can be of real benefit because the interviewer is
sure to make a note of anything significant so that they can
ask you about it later.

Here's a sample answer to the question 'Tell me about
yourself':

'Thank you for seeing me today, and I'm pleased to be able to tell you something about myself. I began my career with The Total Technology Company as a trainee sales representative. I discovered very early on that I had both an aptitude and a liking for sales and after 12 months in that job I progressed to the post of technical sales representative. I worked in the southeast of the country, gaining considerable sales experience, and always achieved the targets for sales turnover and development of new business. After three years in that job, I needed to develop my career and knowledge of the industry, so I moved to the Techno Group as their field sales supervisor. This was an exciting time with considerable growth in the company, and as I'd demonstrated good management skills, particularly those of motivation and teamwork, I was offered my current post, that of sales manager for the UK. I've been in this job for four years and during that time I've restructured the sales team and increased the turnover and profitability of my part of the business.

'As you are aware, an American company has acquired the Techno Group and they plan to amalgamate Techno's UK business with their own. Consequently, my post will be redundant in two months' time, so I'm looking for a new job.

'That's a summary of my background to date. I'm confident that I've all the relevant qualities you require for this job and I'd be happy to expand on any of these points.'

## 2. 'Why are you looking for a job?'

In response to this question, keep your answer short. If you ramble on, the interviewer may suspect that all is not right.

If the job you've applied for is an obvious step up the ladder or is based in a part of the country to which you wish to relocate, you should have no difficulty answering this question. However, there may be many other reasons why you've applied for another job. Perhaps you disliked the work or the boss; maybe there's a risk of redundancy or the company isn't doing well; you may have an unresolved grievance or possibly you'd like to work for a bigger/smaller company. Never say that you disliked your boss; the interviewer may think that you find it difficult to get on with other people. It's far better to say that, although the work is interesting, there's no real opportunity for personal development. Whatever your reason, practise your answer now and don't be caught out unprepared.

### 3. 'What are your strengths?'

This is one of the classic questions that's favoured by many interviewers. Your answer will allow them to compare your strengths with those they have identified as necessary for the job, and they will almost certainly ask you several follow-up questions based on your first response.

The importance of recognising and understanding your personal strengths was explained earlier in this chapter. Include strengths that have played a part in your achievements in your answer. Why? Because the interviewer is certain to ask this follow-up question: 'Can you give me some examples of where you have used these strengths?' Again, prepare yourself for this question and make sure that you can give some concrete examples.

> 'When answering questions about your skills and achievements, always show how you could add value to the company and the job you've applied for.'
>
> *HR manager – computer software manufacturer*

### 4. 'What are your weaknesses?'

No interviewer can resist this question after they've asked you about your strengths. Most candidates find this particular question difficult to answer, either fearing rejection if they admit to any weaknesses or worrying about looking foolish because they can't think of any. Have courage: we're all capable of making mistakes, and most interviewers recognise this.

When you identified your strengths, it was important to take a positive view about improving your weaknesses. In this way, you learn to give a much more confident account of yourself during interviews when asked to reveal your weaknesses.

Revealing your weaknesses in an interview can land you in serious trouble unless you've learned how to transform them into good qualities. The rule is to present your faults positively, or at least render them as inoffensive as possible. In any event, those you offer up should be minor faults that have little influence on your job performance and merit as a potential employee. A list of weaknesses can be found in the skills guide at the back of this book.

One way of answering this type of question is to highlight a weakness that's concerned with job knowledge rather than transferable skills or personal strengths. Make sure the weakness doesn't directly affect your current application: for example, you could say that you haven't yet got to grips with computer software, provided this isn't a key requirement of the job.

It's important to explain how you're attempting to improve this weakness. Give examples, such as training courses attended, further education or help from a more experienced person.

Here's a sample answer to the question 'What are your weaknesses?':

'I have been giving this some thought, because I believe self-development is very important. On a few occasions, I've been too demanding of subordinate staff, usually because I've been targeted to produce something by a specific date. I recognise that this is a weakness and using encouragement, motivation and teamwork I find I can achieve the result I've been looking for.'

## 5. 'What have been your most significant achievements?'

Prepare yourself by looking through your CV to identify achievements that are a good match for the employer's requirements. Employers will be particularly interested in your achievements if you can demonstrate that you have:

- increased sales and profit
- increased new business
- reduced costs
- increased efficiency
- identified and solved problems
- improved systems of management
- improved levels of customer service
- invented a labour-saving or cost-reducing product.

If you're applying for a management post, you should also try to demonstrate that benefit in terms of numbers, money or volume.

Finally, select the two or three most significant achievements and present these in your answer. Here are a couple of examples:

'I increased sales by 127% over a six-year period, and positively contributed to an expansion of the company's market share.'

'I improved telephone-answering response within the customer support department to 15 seconds or less. This increased staff morale and customer satisfaction levels.'

Spend time preparing yourself for follow-up questions. These will usually be along the lines of 'What action did you take to increase sales?' and 'How did you improve the telephone-answering response?'

Another form of this question is 'What have you done that shows initiative?' Employers are very keen on people who can think for themselves and make decisions. Look through your achievements and choose one or two that show how your previous employer benefited from your initiative.

### 6. 'What three words best describe you?'

Sometimes this might be phrased 'How would your last boss describe you?' or 'How would your colleagues at work describe you?' If you've carried out the self-assessment recommended in the first book in this series entitled *Job Search*, and the research suggested earlier in this chapter, you should be able to answer this question. Your efforts will have identified your strengths and those that are the most relevant to this employer.

The real difficulty with this question is choosing just three words from the many you may have identified. Never leave this choice until the interview; it's far better to choose them well in advance. Think about each word carefully and choose one word to describe a transferable skill, one to describe a personal strength and the third to describe specialist knowledge.

Here's a sample answer to the question 'What three words best describe you?': 'Negotiating, creating and managing.'

## 7. 'Why should we offer you this job?'

Another classic question, usually asked towards the end of the interview. The interviewer is asking you how you measure up against the requirements of the job, and whether you have anything really special to offer. Another way of asking this question is 'I've got no further questions, but you've got two minutes to convince me you should have the job.'

To prepare for this question, make sure you've obtained all the information available about the employer and the job. Use the newspaper advertisement, if this is how you first discovered the vacancy, and the job description to identify the employer's requirements. Compare your transferable skills, personal strengths and achievements with these requirements and tell the interviewer where you match and exceed them.

Here's a sample answer to the question 'Why should we offer you this job?':

'I have eight years' experience in a high-pressure sales role and have frequently exceeded sales targets for existing and new business. This, together with my proven ability to acquire new customers and strong negotiating skills, is highly valued by my current employer and I can do it for you.

'I'm particularly skilful at making sales presentations, am computer literate and completely familiar with a wide range of software.

'Finally, because your company is expanding and therefore creating opportunities, my skills and personal strengths of enthusiasm, working well under pressure, loyalty and resourcefulness will help the company achieve its goals.'

## 8. 'Why do you want to work for this company?'

Yet again, this is an opportunity for you to demonstrate to the interviewer what you have learned about the company through your research. Complete your answer by explaining what particularly interests you about the company and why you want to work for them: 'Your company has an excellent reputation in the marketplace for quality products and staff development. This is just the combination of qualities I am looking for in my next employer.'

## 9. 'If I called your last boss, what would they say about you?'

If you've lost your job because of redundancy, expect this question – it's becoming very popular with all types of interviewers. There's only one response worth giving: 'He would re-employ me tomorrow.' Employers select people who they believe will get on well with other people, so even if you didn't like your last boss, never admit it, otherwise this will set alarm bells ringing in the mind of the interviewer.

## 10. 'Do you prefer working on your own or with other people?'

Without knowing enough about the job, you'll find this question difficult to answer. Either preference may lose you the job. It's best to answer the question along the following lines:

'I'm sure that like most other jobs, there will be times when I'm required to work on my own and times when I'll be working with other people. I have no preference, because I enjoy both situations. In my present job I work with three other people, but I've also undertaken project work requiring me to work alone.'

## MYTH BUSTER

### *Most interviewers know what they're looking for*

*Not true! Many interviewers are line managers who have never received any interview training.*

*If line managers don't know what they're looking for, they may well recommend a candidate who's unsuitable for the job or someone just like themselves. This latter failing is known as the 'halo effect'. You may well think that this is unfair, but it happens, so you must be prepared for it.*

*The best way of handling this type of interviewer is to help them by addressing all the employer's requirements contained in the job advertisement. Equally, it's important to make sure that the interviewer appreciates what you've done to prepare for the interview.*

## OTHER QUESTIONS YOU MIGHT BE ASKED

This section contains a sample of the most typical questions you're likely to be asked. Read each question and consider what the interviewer is trying to discover, and then plan your answers using your list of transferable skills, personal strengths and achievements.

# OTHER QUESTIONS YOU MIGHT BE ASKED

1. Why have you been in your current/last job for such a long time?
2. What mistakes have you made and what have you learned from them?
3. Tell me about a time when you had to go beyond what's ordinarily expected of an employee in order to get the job done.
4. In what way has your job prepared you to take on greater responsibility?
5. Why do you feel you'll be successful in this work?
6. What experience have you had working as part of a team?
7. What kinds of problems do you handle best?
8. What qualities should a successful manager possess?
9. What's your style of leadership?
10. How do you motivate people?
11. What have you learned from your mistakes?
12. You seem to have had a lot of job moves – why?
13. What do you dislike about your current job?
14. Why did you leave your last job?
15. What are your plans for your own personal development?
16. Why do you feel you're ready to take on greater responsibility?
17. How long do you think it would take before you could make a contribution to this company?
18. What have you learned about yourself as a result of being redundant?
19. Tell me about the most difficult subordinate you've had to deal with.
20. How do you organise yourself to ensure things get done on time?
21. Do you often work late to finish your tasks?
22. Why are you prepared to work for less money than you were previously earning?
23. What do you know about this company?
24. How do you communicate with your staff?
25. How do you build morale?
26. Tell me about a project you initiated.
27. What are your team-player qualities?
28. What sort of training would you need to do this job well?
29. Are you willing to relocate?
30. Have you any positions of responsibility outside work?

# EXAMPLES OF QUESTIONS ASKED OF RECENT UNIVERSITY GRADUATES

1. What factors affected your choice of university?
2. Why did you choose to study (subject title)?
3. Tell me about your thesis.
4. Are these the best grades you could have achieved?
5. How have your educational and work experiences prepared you for this job?
6. How have you spent your vacations during your time at university?
7. Tell me about your summer jobs.
8. Who was your favourite lecturer and why?
9. Why didn't you have a temporary job during the summer vacation?
10. Were you involved in any extra-curricular activities?
11. Which lecturing styles appealed to you most and why?
12. How have you changed personally since being at university?
13. Why have you chosen this particular profession?
14. What criteria are you using to evaluate the company for which you hope to work?
15. How has your university course prepared you for a business career?
16. Are you willing to spend at least 12 months as a trainee?

## QUESTIONS YOU SHOULD ASK THE EMPLOYER

Once the interviewer has come to the end of their questions, they'll usually ask if you have any questions you'd like to ask. Some candidates don't prepare for this part of the interview; consequently, they panic and usually ask a few ridiculous questions that merely fill an otherwise embarrassing silence.

Interviewers are interested in the questions you ask, because they provide an opportunity for you to demonstrate your knowledge of the company and show an interest in the job you've applied for. Obviously, you need to prepare some questions in advance, but you must also be ready to ask new questions that reflect the information obtained throughout the interview. This will almost certainly happen in a conversational interview, when you may be given a lot of information about the company and the job. Here are some guidelines to help you construct suitable questions:

- Ask a maximum of three questions. However, it's important that you don't prolong the interview beyond the stage at which the interviewer wishes to finish. If you've given lengthy answers to the interviewer's questions, you won't help your cause by dragging out the interview by asking too many questions.
- Don't ask about anything you should already know from information previously supplied by the company, such as job description, annual report, etc.
- Ask questions that demonstrate to the employer that you're interested in their objectives, problems, needs and concerns.
- Don't ask about salary and benefits. These questions are best left until you receive an offer.
- Structure your questions so that the interviewer is left in no doubt that you've carried out some research about the company.
- Make sure you have a good understanding of the job and the responsibilities. If this hasn't been made clear during the interview, ask appropriate questions.
- Adopt a conversational style with your questions that lets the interviewer know you've something to contribute.

Here is a list of questions you can ask the employer:

# QUESTIONS YOU CAN
# ASK DURING AN INTERVIEW

- Where does this position fit into your overall organisation?
- To whom would I report?
- Is there anything unusually demanding about the job I should know about?
- What do you see as the priorities for someone in this position?
- Is there a typical career path for a person in this position?
- How are employees evaluated and promoted?
- What type of on-the-job training is available?
- Does the job involve travel? If so, how much?
- Does your company encourage its employees to undertake further education and training?
- What are the company's plans for the future?
- What are the biggest challenges facing the company?

# A USEFUL PREPARATION EXERCISE

Here's a useful exercise that brings together all the elements of interview preparation:

1. Describe five transferable skills, personal strengths and achievements that you think would appeal most to an employer.
2. Describe your ideal working environment. This includes the physical environment, the kind of company and its culture, the type of people with whom you'd like to work, the amount of supervision and direction.
3. Describe what you know about the company, the industry and the position in which you're interested.
4. Describe your own educational background and explain how it's relevant to the position in which you're interested.
5. Describe how your background and experience are relevant to the position in which you're interested.
6. Describe your career goals and how they relate to this position.
7. What are your weaknesses and what steps are you taking to improve them?
8. What questions do you want to ask the interviewer?

# Case Study

# Interview preparation

Gary Newton was made redundant from his job as a sales representative at the age of 45. Relatives and friends warned him to expect a long time out of work, because many employers would consider him too old to join their workforce. Gary's reaction was one of disbelief, but he realised that he'd have to work hard at convincing an employer he was the right person for their job.

In the next few weeks, Gary made use of his network of contacts, arranging meetings and applying for suitable jobs advertised in national newspapers.

Although he received quite a few rejection letters, he also received invitations to two sets of interviews. Gary was used to putting in a lot of time researching potential customers, so he understood just how important this is when it comes to job interviews. 'I set about asking for copies of the company's annual report and product leaflets and found quite a lot of useful information on the Internet and in my local library. I'm used to talking to people of all levels, but I accepted that my interview skills were in need of improvement, so I listed the questions they were most likely to ask and rehearsed my answers.'

'On the day of each interview, I was so pleased that I'd undertaken some research. The interviewers asked me quite a few questions that were obviously geared to determine what I knew about the company. I felt very pleased with my interview performance.'

One week later Gary received a letter stating he'd been shortlisted by one employer, and a letter from the second employer offering him a job. He was delighted with the outcome and decided to accept the offer of employment.

# REMEMBER

✔ Interviewers place a great deal of importance on preparation and will soon be able to tell whether you've prepared for an interview or if you're bluffing.

✔ The first step in preparing yourself for interviews is self-assessment. By focusing on your transferable skills, personal strengths and achievements, and not your weaknesses, you'll be able to accentuate the positive and eliminate the negative.

✔ Familiarise yourself with the position you've applied for.

✔ Familiarise yourself with the employer.

✔ Familiarise yourself with the industry you'll be working in.

✔ Using your list of transferable skills, personal strengths and achievements, prepare your own answers to the ten most common interview questions on pages 28 to 36.

✔ Read each of the interview questions on pages 37 to 38. Consider what the interviewer is trying to discover and then plan your answers.

✔ Interviewers are interested in the questions you ask, because they provide an opportunity for you to demonstrate your knowledge of the company and show an interest in the job you've applied for.

✔ Prepare some questions in advance of the interview, but also be ready to ask new questions that reflect the information obtained throughout the interview.

✔ Practise the useful exercise on page 40, bringing together all the elements of interview preparation.

Body language

## FIRST IMPRESSIONS

It's often said that interviewers make their decisions in the first four minutes of the interview, and then spend the rest of the time looking for information that supports that decision.

First impressions are based on your appearance, how you conduct yourself and, to a much smaller extent, what you actually say. The interviewer unconsciously compares you with their 'ideal candidate' based on their own personal set of values and almost certainly some prejudices. This happens because the brain reacts instinctively on an emotional level before it can begin to analyse any information. If your appearance seems to contradict what you're saying, the interviewer will be inclined to disbelieve what you say, because the visual message is much stronger. From their viewpoint, a well-groomed, appropriately dressed and confident candidate will get off to a better start than someone who doesn't present themselves so well, irrespective of what they actually say. Of course, this can often lead to bad judgement on the interviewer's part, but that's why it's so important to manage every moment of your interview, particularly the critical first few minutes.

## APPEARANCE

When you dress for your interview, you want to look credible, successful and confident. Choosing to wear casual clothes normally associated with leisure activities may convey to the interviewer that you don't take your career seriously. Choosing to dress professionally conveys to the interviewer that you take pride in your appearance, and that you appreciate the importance of the job for which you're applying.

To be well dressed you must wear clothes that:

- complement you physically
- express your personality
- are appropriate for the occasion, and
- are current but not necessarily in the height of fashion.

Clothes that complement you physically complement your colouring and bodyline: a good fit makes the difference between an expensive, tailored look and an inexpensive, inappropriate appearance. To express your personality your clothes should look as if they belong to you. Dress appropriately for the job in question, adopting a similar style to that worn by the interviewers. For most interviews, this would usually mean formal or business attire. However, if you're attending an interview for the job of a machine operator or motor mechanic, for example, you may well be interviewed by someone wearing an overall. This doesn't mean you have an excuse to wear jeans, sloppy jumper and trainers. If you decide that a suit is inappropriate, make sure that you choose something smart and not brightly coloured.

## Men

Men should wear a suit in a dark material – dark grey and navy are the most acceptable – accompanied by a high-contrast coloured shirt (white or cream) for the high impact authoritative look. Alternatively, wear a suit in a lighter coloured material with a low-contrast coloured shirt for that friendly and approachable look. Pinstripes are acceptable provided the stripes are narrow. It's wise to invest in the quality and fit of your suit, so choose 100% wool, because this looks and wears better.

Wear a formal tie and not a flashy one. It should complement your suit and be no wider than the width of your suit lapels. Don't wear ties that have pictures of cartoon figures or sporting symbols – keep them for social occasions! The tie should extend to your trouser belt and the knot should be neat.

Complete the outfit with a pair of freshly shined black or brown leather shoes. Socks should be black, dark grey or navy. Make sure that shoes and socks complement the rest of your clothes.

Keep jewellery to an absolute minimum and always remove earrings. Finally, be sure you're well groomed and that your hairstyle is businesslike, conservative and clean-cut.


## Women

Women don't have to copy the male uniform. They can express their individuality while still looking completely professional. If possible, choose something that's businesslike, yet currently in style. There are no hard and fast rules, but a skirt with a well-tailored and stylish jacket in a solid darker colour is preferable. However, an outfit comprising skirt or dress in a solid colour with a co-ordinating jacket is acceptable. Some people still find trousers unacceptable female apparel so play safe and stick to a skirt or dress, unless you feel strongly on the subject. Avoid strong bright colours and aim for materials that retain their shape. The sensitive use of colour is a powerful business tool. You'll project credibility, and look healthier and attractive, if you choose the colours with care and your outfit fits well.

Blouses made from natural fabrics are preferable, because they absorb moisture better than synthetic fabrics. Keep to solid colours if you can, and choose one that complements the rest of your outfit. Wear comfortable leather shoes in the same colour or a slightly darker shade than your skirt or dress.

Your hair should be neatly styled. The natural look with cosmetics is recommended, and your nails should be neatly manicured. If you want to wear nail polish, choose a restrained colour that complements your complete outfit. It's best not to wear perfume because this can be very off-putting for some interviewers. If you choose to wear earrings, make sure they are small and don't attract attention.

> 'It's a good idea to try on the clothes you intend to wear several days before the interview. Check them for lost buttons, stains, and whether they need dry cleaning or pressing. This could save you a great deal of embarrassment on the day of the interview.'
> *Graduate recruitment manager – retail DIY*

## FEELING GOOD ABOUT YOURSELF

Almost everyone knows that the way you dress can influence people, and we often think that our appearance is the most obvious symbol of our image. However, although an expensive business suit will certainly help to create a good first impression, it's up to you to communicate confidence. Our true image is communicated by our self-esteem or how we see ourselves, rather than a reflection of how others see us. A poor self-image can inhibit your ability to relate to other people and communicate effectively. On the other hand, a good self-image raises your level of self-esteem and can fill you full of confidence. Sure of your values and principles, you won't spend time worrying about mistakes or being upset if your job application is rejected. Most important of all, you'll feel good about yourself, confident that you're a person of interest and value to employers.

You can improve your self-esteem by taking a realistic look at yourself. Begin this process by acknowledging that you receive both positive and negative messages about yourself. However, it's the negative messages that really make an impression on your self-esteem. Deal with this by reinforcing the positive messages and by telling yourself that you're a caring, intelligent and positive person. Look at your list of transferable skills, personal strengths and achievements – what do these say about you? Remind yourself about the hard work all of this involved. Focus on your strengths and not your weaknesses, accentuate the positive and eliminate the negative. Take pride in your accomplishments and achievements, no matter how small.

Anxiety during interviews often stems from poor self-esteem caused by the recollection of past negative experiences. These feelings may prevail until you can replace them with a few new, positive experiences. Breaking the habit of being fearful takes a little practice. Fear is a powerful emotion, because it feeds on the possibility of failure. What if you make a mess of everything you have planned and rehearsed?

Here's a simple technique that will help you to relax. When you're introduced to the interviewer, grasp the initiative: rather than taking a seat and waiting for that first question – the one that would feed your anxiety – ask the interviewer a question about something you were unable to discover during your research. For example: 'I notice that you're opening a new office. Is the company expanding?' or 'I'd like to make sure that I cover everything that's important to you. How do you intend to structure the interview?'

These few minutes, during which the interviewer answers your questions, will help you to relax and make you realise that the interviewer actually wants you to do well. Your interest in what the interviewer is saying will soon take over, as you join in the conversation and feel your confidence beginning to grow. This small success can considerably reduce your anxiety, and is precisely the sort of positive message your self-esteem needs. Reinforce this positive message by telling yourself that you've made a good start to the interview, and you should feel your anxiety slip away.

> 'First impressions are very important. In the first four or five minutes, the interviewer is bombarded with all kinds of signals from the candidate. These include the suitability of what the candidate is wearing, body language and verbal communication. It may not seem fair, but these impressions tend to be lasting impressions.'
>
> *Recruitment manager – insurance industry*

## NON-VERBAL COMMUNICATION

During communication, other people rely more on our body language than what we actually say to form a judgement about us. Our posture, gesture and facial expressions are constantly sending out messages. These messages make very powerful statements about who we are, how we're feeling and what we're thinking.

Body language, or non-verbal communication, accounts for about 70% of what we communicate, with tone of voice and the actual words we use making up the other 30%. It can either reinforce your verbal messages or discount them, and it's often the basis on which people decide whether or not you're worth listening to.

If you're not in control of your body language, you may find that what you intend to say is interpreted very differently by those observing your body language. For example, in a stressful situation such as an interview, our bodies may send out positive or negative signals. If our body language complements our verbal responses, then our message is positively reinforced. However, when our body language contradicts what we say, the interviewer may begin to doubt our genuineness. This ability to read another person's non-verbal cues and to compare them with verbal signals is sometimes called intuition or perceptiveness.

Body language is influenced by self-perception, in the same way as self-esteem. Just as you can improve your self-esteem by changing your self-perception, you can correct any negative body language by understanding your transferable skills, personal strengths, values, and taking pride in your achievements. Appropriate control and use of your body language can help you emphasise the positive aspects of your personality and will reinforce the messages you wish to convey to the interviewer. Understanding the interviewer's body language can also help you to identify the occasions when it might be a good idea to adjust your interview strategy.

If you're having difficulty appreciating how non-verbal communication can convey a meaning all of its own, imagine for one moment how the stars of the silent movies handled their screen roles without verbal communication. The most successful actors were those who were able to convey to their audience the story line using only gestures, facial expressions and other body signals. Totally deaf people also become highly skilled at 'reading' non-verbal communication.

To practise interpreting body language, set aside ten minutes a day to examine people's gestures. Turn the sound down on your television and watch all the non-verbal signals. Turn the sound up again after a few minutes to determine how accurate your interpretation has been.

## Greeting the interviewer

Greeting the interviewer begins with the handshake. However, it's best not to initiate this yourself, because it may convey a desire to dominate the interview. The best approach is to respond quickly when the interviewer offers their hand in greeting.

It's possible to tell quite a lot from a handshake. When the palm of the hand is facing downwards, this indicates a dominant attitude. In a variation of this, the arm is kept stiff to keep the other person at a distance, and is associated with the knuckle grinder or tough guy approach. A submissive attitude is demonstrated by keeping the palm of your hand facing upwards. Sometimes this can be associated with the limp and clammy dead-fish handshake.

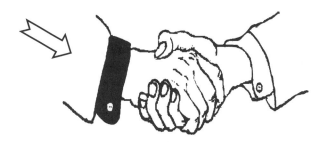

*Figure 1 – The dominant handshake*

*Figure 2 – The knuckle grinder*

*Figure 3 – The submissive handshake*

*Figure 4 – A positive and co-operative handshake*

For obvious reasons, don't use any of these handshakes when greeting an interviewer. Instead, make sure your hands are clean, warm and free of perspiration. Keep the palm of your hand vertical and grip the interviewer's hand firmly. Try to match the pressure exerted by the interviewer, but never exceed it. Maintain eye contact and a warm smile. This approach will signal co-operation, respect and friendliness.

## Seating

Wait for the interviewer to offer you a chair, but if you feel uncomfortable, take the initiative and ask where they would like you to sit. A lot has been written about the dangers of encroaching on another person's personal space, so make sure the chair is no closer than 1.2 metres from the interviewer's seating position. Sit with your bottom well back in the chair, keep your back straight and adopt a comfortable posture without slouching.

## Arm gestures

When people feel nervous, negative or defensive, most will exhibit a particular universal non-verbal gesture, folding their arms firmly across their chest to signal that they feel threatened. Known as the closed body or closed attitude position, it's a strong signal to an interviewer that something is wrong.

Some people claim that they simply fold their arms because it's the most comfortable position. However, it's important to understand that whilst they may feel comfortable with their arms crossed, the person receiving this gesture will interpret it as negative.

## Hand gestures

Many people seem to have little or no control of their hands, particularly in a stressful situation such as an interview. Common problems include fidgeting with rings, watches, cufflinks and pens. Whilst these gestures are an attempt to conceal nervousness and are annoying to the interviewer, there are other negative gestures that are much more harmful to your chances of achieving interview success.

As a child, in an attempt to stifle words of deceit, we would cover our mouths with our hands, thumbs pressed against the cheek. Known as the mouth guard, this gesture remains with us in adulthood.

Whilst there may be variations on the mouth guard gesture, they all mean the same thing – that the speaker is almost certainly telling a lie. Other non-verbal gestures of deceit include lightly rubbing your face below the nose, rubbing the eye and pulling the collar away from the neck. Interview candidates who put their fingers in their mouth are signalling that they are under pressure and need reassurance.

Practise a neutral position for your hands; keep them resting on your knees, but don't be tempted to clench your hands together.

## Leg gestures

Crossed legs, like crossed arms, are often seen as signalling a negative or defensive attitude. Locking the ankles has the same meaning. Avoid annoying habits such as tapping the floor with the toe end of your shoes or shuffling your feet under the chair. Distracting the interviewer in this way will almost certainly mean they miss or ignore your important verbal statements.

## Face and eyes

Whilst most parts of the body are capable of sending out positive and negative signals, the face, and particularly the eyes and mouth, are the most expressive. Since most interviewers will aim to maintain eye contact with candidates, any non-verbal facial signals are likely to be noted.

When a candidate is holding back information, their eyes are likely to meet the interviewer's gaze less than one-third of the time. This lack of eye contact may also indicate nervousness and timidity, but the person receiving this gesture will still interpret it as a negative gesture. However, one word of warning: how long you maintain eye contact is determined by culture, so don't be too quick to jump to conclusions.

Raised eyebrows and a 'O'-shaped open mouth signify surprise, whilst raised eyebrows and an open smile indicate real pleasure. Knotted eyebrows and a downturned mouth suggest sadness, whilst tightly pursed lips are a sign of displeasure. Speaking with the eyes closed for a second or so is known as the eye block gesture. This is an attempt by the person to block you from their sight, because they're not particularly interested in what you have to say. From an interviewer's viewpoint, this is a most irritating negative gesture.

Eye contact is very important during an interview. The dangers of avoiding eye contact have already been mentioned, but it's also possible to overdo eye contact. If this becomes too intense, it may well be interpreted as an aggressive gesture and only succeed in making the interviewer feel uncomfortable. Aim for moderate eye contact – roughly 70% of the time – and occasionally break your gaze to look at your CV or something on the interviewer's desk. This indicates sincerity and conveys the impression that you're paying attention.

Your smile can be a powerful positive body signal. Used selectively to reinforce other positive signals, both verbal and non-verbal, you'll appear confident, friendly and relaxed.

## MYTH BUSTER

### *I understand that it may be possible to fake body language*

*It's extremely difficult to fake body language without giving yourself away at some point. Whilst you're trying to cover up one particular gesture, other gestures are telling a different story. However, this doesn't mean that you can't learn to eliminate negative gestures and associate positive gestures with positive verbal communication.*

## CLEARLY, THE WAY TO TALK

Whilst interview success can hinge on what you say, how you say it is also very important. The most common problems are mumbling, grating timbres and a dull monotone. Less common, but just as harmful in an interview, is a voice that's artificially high or spoken through clenched teeth.

It's easy to overlook the powerful effect a voice can have in determining the outcome of an interview. The best way to test this is to listen to a tape-recording of your voice. If you spot any of these problems, practise speaking so that your voice is clear, reflects warmth and enthusiasm and has a pleasing tone.

Here are ten steps towards better body language:

1.  **Posture.** Sloppy posture conveys a lack of confidence and, possibly, a lack of discipline. When you meet your contact, stand erect with your shoulders back and you'll convey an alert and enthusiastic manner.

2.  **Handshakes.** Shake hands firmly keeping the palm of the hand in the vertical position and don't hold the contact for too long.

3.  **Seating.** Make sure you're comfortably seated. Keep your back straight, unbutton your jacket and relax your breathing.

4.  **Eye contact.** Eyes are an important aspect of body language and are crucial in establishing rapport. Make eye contact before you speak and when your contact is speaking. Aim for maintaining contact about 70% of the time, and look away occasionally to avoid staring.

5.  **Comfort zone.** People have a comfort zone that dictates how close they want other people to come, particularly when seated. Never invade your contact's space unless invited.

6.  **Hands and arms.** Most problems with hands are due to nervousness. Don't keep your hands in your pocket or fidget with rings, watches or cufflinks. Keep your hands away from your face. Don't put your hands behind your head. Avoid folding your arms across your chest; it's best to keep them on the arms of the chair. If there are no arms on your chair, then try resting your hands on your knees, but don't be tempted to clench your hands together.

7.  **Leg gestures.** Crossed legs, like crossed arms, are often seen as a negative or defensive posture.

Adopt a comfortable seating position, keeping your legs together and both feet on the ground without locking your ankles.

8. **Nodding agreement.** Using nods to punctuate key remarks made by the other person will signal agreement, interest and understanding.

9. **Smiling.** Smiling is a positive signal and projects warmth. Most people look better when they smile, and it will make your contacts more comfortable because you'll appear natural and confident.

10. **Voice.** Listen to a tape-recording of your voice and practise speaking so that your voice is clear, reflects warmth and enthusiasm and has a pleasing tone.

Having a clear understanding of body language helps you to avoid negative non-verbal signals, replacing them, whenever possible, with open positive body signals that reinforce your verbal communication. Controlling your body language in this way can only improve your chances of interview success.

## Case Study
## Body language

When asked by the recruitment consultant why he was leaving his current job, Bob, an experienced office manager, replied without hesitation, 'Opportunities for promotion are very limited.' Not satisfied with his response, the consultant continued to probe until Bob finally admitted that a difference of opinion with the finance director over department staffing led to his resignation. After the interview, Bob wondered what he had said that prompted the consultant to pursue the issue. Bob didn't realise that his verbal response wasn't the problem. Rather, his body language suggested that he wasn't being completely frank and open.

Until that point in the interview, Bob had been sitting quite comfortably with his legs together and both feet on the ground. His hands were resting in his lap and his eyes were focused directly on the consultant's face. When the question about leaving his current employer arose, Bob unconsciously shifted in his seat, crossed his left leg over his right, leaned forward slightly and placed his hands on the desk in front of him. The specific gestures were of no particular significance; however, changes in his body language were enough to suggest to the consultant that he wasn't being completely honest.

# REMEMBER

✔ First impressions are based on your appearance, how you conduct yourself (body language) and to a much smaller extent what you actually say.

✔ Clothes that complement you physically complement your colouring and bodyline.

✔ Dress appropriately for the job in question, adopting a similar style to that worn by the interviewers.

✔ Our true image is communicated by how we see ourselves, rather than a reflection of how others see us.

✔ A good self-image raises your level of self-esteem and can fill you full of confidence.

✔ To relax at the start of an interview, grasp the initiative and ask a question about something you were unable to discover during your research.

✔ Other people rely more on our body language than what we actually say to form a judgement about us.

✔ To practise interpreting body language, set aside ten minutes a day to examine other people's gestures.

✔ If you avoid using negative non-verbal signals and reinforce your verbal communication with open positive body signals, this can only improve your chances of interview success.

✔ Whilst interview success can hinge on what you say, how you say it is also very important.

## ON THE DAY OF THE INTERVIEW

The time has come for your interview, and by now you should be well prepared. Here is some general advice to help you with your interview performance:

- Always allow plenty of time to get to the interview. The last thing you want to do is arrive with a few minutes to spare feeling anxious and out of breath. Aim to be ten minutes early. However, if you arrive too early, use the opportunity to take a walk around the block to focus your thoughts. You'll find that this will help you to relax.
- Report to reception, and remember to be polite and friendly to the receptionist. If possible, try to strike up a conversation: this person may be a source of useful information. If there's a cloakroom handy, pay a visit to check out your hair and general appearance.
- Whilst you're waiting, take a good look around and try to form an impression of the company.
- Remember the importance of the first four minutes. This is where you'll make your first impression.
- Smile confidently as you walk into the room. Make eye contact but don't stare.
- Greet the interviewer enthusiastically and introduce yourself. Shake hands firmly. (To avoid a wet handshake induced by nerves, wipe your hands on a handkerchief before entering the room.)
- Don't chew gum or smoke.
- Don't sit down until you're invited to do so.

- Be aware of your body language: sit upright in your chair and look alert and interested at all times. Keep both feet on the ground. Don't fold your arms. Show that you can be an intelligent listener as well as a talker. Don't let your hands betray your nervousness. If you don't know where to put them, leave them in your lap and keep them still.

- Take your CV with you, but don't put this on the interviewer's desk; instead, leave it on the floor next to your chair. If you must take your briefcase, only include the paperwork you need for the interview. This way you won't panic when the interviewer asks for your CV.

- Don't take notes during the interview: some interviewers find this annoying and distracting.

- Remember, you can deal with anxiety by asking the interviewer a question about something you were unable to discover during your research.

- Maintain a positive attitude throughout the interview. This is by far the best way to control your nerves. If you've done all your preparation, and think positively about yourself, your skills, personal qualities and achievements, you'll have nothing to worry about.

- Use frequent, direct eye contact with the interviewer, especially when responding to questions.

- Always answer the question. You may consider this rather obvious, but it's a very common mistake. Many candidates simply don't listen to the question properly and give an irrelevant answer. So, listen carefully to what the interviewer asks. If you're at all unsure of the question, ask the interviewer for more information.

- Make sure everything you say is relevant. Don't stray away from the question or topic of conversation.

- Take time to think your answer through. Rushing in too quickly can often result in an ill-thought-out response. Pause before answering and give yourself time to collect your thoughts together.

- Never answer a question with a simple 'Yes' or 'No'. As explained in Chapter 2, closed questions are framed to draw out just this response. Begin your answer with 'Yes' or 'No', but always include a full explanation. Here's an example:

**Interviewer:** *'Can you operate a computer?'*
**Candidate:** *'Yes, I've attended several IT training courses and I'm very familiar with most word-processing, desk-top publishing and spreadsheet software. In addition, I've worked with both Internet and intranet applications.'*

- Speak up confidently when answering questions, and let your personality shine through.
- Never exaggerate or give dishonest answers; it simply doesn't pay.
- Whenever possible use specific examples to illustrate or 'prove' your strengths to the interviewer.
- Don't take a defensive attitude when discussing weaknesses. An apologetic approach won't win you any points. Instead, accentuate the positive by identifying what you've learned from your mistakes.
- When answering any question, try to make a clear connection between yourself and the job you've applied for. Use your experience, transferable skills and personal strengths to prove you're the best candidate for the job.
- Be prepared for hypothetical situation questions and take your time answering them. Try to imagine yourself in that situation. If it's a situation that you haven't already experienced, give the best answer you can. In many instances, the interviewer is more interested in finding out how you'd react under those circumstances, and in your thinking processes, than in your final answer.

- Don't use jargon or acronyms specific to a job or industry with which the interviewer may not be familiar.
- Never talk money until you know there's a job offer. You may be naturally curious about salary and benefits, but resist the urge to ask about it during the interview. If you do, the interviewer may well conclude that you appear more concerned with what you can get out of the job than with what you can contribute.
- Answer all questions with enthusiasm, even those that seem entirely irrelevant to the job. Questions about current events, for example, can often tell the interviewer something about your personality that may not be revealed during your answers to more straightforward questions.
- Never lose your patience with the interviewer, even if their style isn't to your liking.
- Don't make disparaging remarks about your present or previous employer. Such remarks won't help your cause, and it will only seem that you're blaming others for your own shortcomings.

'A common rule known by sales people is that enthusiasm for their product or service is 50% of the sale. In this case, the product you're selling is yourself. Be enthusiastic about your skills and what you've accomplished. This won't be interpreted as arrogance. Genuine enthusiasm is contagious and can play a large part in getting an offer of employment.'

*Graduate recruitment manager – food manufacturer*

- Don't give ambiguous answers such as 'I think I could do the job', 'Maybe', 'Probably' or 'I imagine so'. These answers lack the impact of 'Certainly', 'Definitely' and 'Yes'.
- Don't use diluted language. Phrases such as 'and stuff', 'or something', 'you know', and 'sort of' sound unprofessional and ineffective, and only diffuse what is otherwise a confident message.

- Show interest in what the interviewer has to say about the job and the company. Let them know through your answers that you really want the job.
- Summarise and have a positive approach. Be certain to thank the interviewer for their time and consideration. Resist the temptation to flatter them; you'll be misunderstood. Smile and show as much confidence when you leave as you did on your arrival.

## MYTH BUSTER

### *The first candidate in a set of interviews is at a disadvantage*

*Not true! There's no evidence to support this view. On the day of the interviews, the employer is most likely to select the candidate who performs the best.*

## EVALUATING YOUR INTERVIEW PERFORMANCE

After the interview has ended, you'll probably feel a sense of relief. The temptation then is to relax and forget everything that happened. However, if you want to learn anything from the experience, and so improve your interview technique, it's important to evaluate your performance whilst the event is still fresh in your mind.

Sit down with pen and paper, and list what went well and what went badly. Try to recall *why* some aspects of the interview weren't successful. List all the questions you had difficulty answering. Could you have stressed your skills, strengths and achievements more than you did? Were you in control of your body language? Did you create an opportunity to demonstrate your research and preparation?

To help you with this, use the format employed in the interview evaluation form below.

'It's important to look back over your interview for any negatives – these are aspects of your performance that need to be improved if you're to succeed in future interviews.'
*Personnel and training manager – entertainment industry*

## INTERVIEW EVALUATION FORM

Interview date:
Company name:
Interviewer's name:

1.  Describe your overall performance at the interview:


2.  Questions that were difficult to answer:


3.  Did you make the interviewer fully aware of your transferable skills, personal strengths and achievements? If not, why not?


4.  Were you in control of your body language? How could this be improved?


5.  Did you ask sensible, relevant questions?


6.  Were you adequately prepared for this interview? What can be done to improve any areas of weakness?


7.  What else would you do to improve your performance at the next interview?

## CREATING A LASTING IMPRESSION

Immediately you've completed your interview evaluation, and provided you're really interested in the job, send the interviewer a short letter of appreciation. Begin by thanking them for the interview and for telling you about the job and the company. Explain that you're very interested in the post and remind them of what you can contribute in terms of key skills and personal strengths.

Send this letter within 24 hours of the interview and address it to the senior interviewer.

## REMEMBER

✔ Study the advice about interview performance in this chapter. Arriving in good time for the interview, making a good entrance *and* creating a good first impression are all important factors. Be aware of your body language and keep anxiety at bay. Be positive throughout the interview, take time to think up relevant answers, and reflect your transferable skills, personal strengths and achievements. Be prepared to deal with hypothetical questions and summarise using a positive approach.

✔ When the interview has ended, if you wish to learn from the experience and improve your interview performance, the process of evaluation is very important.

✔ Send a letter of appreciation to the senior interviewer within 24 hours of the interview.

## 6 Dealing with job offers and rejection

## SUCCESS AT LAST

Congratulations! If you've been offered the ideal job, and by ideal, I mean one that feels right for you with the anticipated pay and benefits, then you should be feeling on top of the world. However, never jump into making an immediate career decision. Take time to analyse the job offer carefully. Weigh all the positives and negatives, and compare them with what you want out of a job. In particular, consider the following:

- Does the company live up to your expectations? Is it expanding or contracting? Is the company style or culture right for you? What clues did you get from the interviewer?
- Take a careful look at the job description, the job advertisement and your interview evaluation form. Are the duties and responsibilities what you expected?
- Is there sufficient opportunity for career development?
- Will you be able to continue in further education? Will the company support you financially with this?
- Are you happy with your place of work? Will you be required to travel or stay away from home?
- Is the salary generous enough? How often will your salary be reviewed? Will this review be based on your job performance?
- Are the benefits what you expected? If a company car is provided, is this fully expensed by the company?
- If accepting the job means you have to move area, have you been offered assistance with relocation?

- Consider other benefits such as pension, sickness payments, health insurance, hours of work and period of notice.
- Does the company have a 'no smoking' policy?
- What kind of image does the quality of the contract documentation convey?

If the documentation you've received is unclear on any of these topics, you should contact the personnel manager or recruitment consultant and ask for clarification. If the offer is not quite right – maybe the salary is less than you hoped for – make sure you know what to expect from future salary reviews. If, on balance, you still believe the company is undervaluing you, you could try a little negotiation to bring about an improvement. At this stage, the interviewer is vulnerable, because they've spent a great deal of time and effort in selecting you as the best candidate. They certainly won't want to begin the recruitment and selection process all over again. Pluck up courage and make contact with the interviewer. Tell them that you'd like to accept the offer, but the salary is less than you expected. An experienced interviewer will take this in their stride and may ask you what salary you were expecting, so be prepared with an answer. All being well, this gentle pressure should work in your favour.

'If you're planning to negotiate with an employer, it's best to work out your minimum cash requirements before doing so. This entails knowing how much you need to maintain a reasonable standard of living. You can then use this figure as the basis for what you need and what you're worth when you enter discussions with the employer.'

Specialist recruitment consultant – Southeast

If, after careful consideration, you decide to decline the offer, send a suitably worded letter to the employer. Here's a sample letter:

Tel: 01865 023178

34 Norfolk Gardens
South Kingston
Oxford OX5 9LL

25 September 2000

Mr Gavin Yates
Managing Director
Wessex Office Supplies
67–69 Dorset Road
Oxford OX7 8QQ

Dear Mr Yates

<u>Accounts Supervisor</u>

Thank you so much for your recent letter offering me the post of Accounts Supervisor.

I've considered your offer very carefully and, as you're aware, I've had a very helpful discussion with Mr Jones, your personnel manager. Regrettably, I must decline your offer as I feel this isn't the job for me.

The salary offered was only slightly more than my current salary and, taking into account the likely date for my next salary review, this doesn't meet my current expectations. In addition, I don't believe that I'd be advancing my career if I were to accept your offer.

Thank you again for your time and consideration.

Yours sincerely

*June Miller*

June Miller

## LEAVING YOUR CURRENT EMPLOYER

If you've formally accepted an offer of employment and you're currently employed, you will have to tender your resignation in writing. Even if you thoroughly dislike your current employer, you should aim to leave them on good terms. Give them the full period of notice to which they're entitled, avoid taking holiday entitlement as part of your notice period and try to make your departure from the company as smooth as possible. This is a demonstration of your loyalty and courtesy and anything less may affect the terms of your departure. Never forget that your new employer will contact your current employer for a reference.

## HANDLING REJECTION

When you receive letters of rejection, it's quite normal to feel disappointment. However, it's important that you shouldn't dwell on this for too long. Think of it instead as a learning experience and then rise above your disappointment. Only if you do this will you be able to get on with your life and maintain the confidence you need to succeed.

Some career specialists suggest contacting the interviewer to ask for feedback or at least a reason for the rejection. This isn't recommended, because it's highly unlikely that you'll get a helpful reply. If every candidate did this, the interviewer would be spending a great deal of time on this unproductive activity. So, you can perhaps understand why asking for feedback is unpopular with most interviewers.

Instead of asking for feedback, why not send a short letter thanking the interviewer and asking to be considered for any similar vacancies that may arise. Here's a sample letter:

Tel: 0161 787 888

129 Roman Road
Homefield
Manchester
N22 8YD

17 December 2000

Mr David Hartley
Recruitment and Development Manager
Micro Computer Company Ltd
66 Hardcastle Road
Manchester M67 7TT

Dear Mr Hartley

<u>Computer Programmer – Ref. MCC3Q</u>

Thank you for your recent letter informing me that my application for the post of Computer Programmer has been unsuccessful.

Naturally, I was disappointed in not being chosen for this post. However, I'd like to say how much I enjoyed the visit to your company and in particular the time taken to introduce me to your senior IT staff.

I should be grateful if you'd keep my CV and consider me for any similar vacancies in the future.

Kind regards

*Peter Smith*

Peter Smith

> 'Never take rejection personally. This is a sure-fire way to end up feeling sorry for yourself. See rejection as being a step nearer to that all-important offer of employment. If it's possible to identify what may have let you down during the interview, then take positive steps to remedy this.'
>
> *General manager – travel industry*

The most positive way of dealing with rejection is to look again at the information recorded on your interview evaluation form. What did you identify that could lead to an improvement in your interview performance? Have you taken steps to improve these aspects of your performance?

It's important to remain positive and optimistic throughout the process of job search and interviews. As an optimist you'll learn from the experience, bounce back with a fresh approach, look for solutions and form a plan for improvement.

## MYTH BUSTER

*The reason most people are rejected after attending an interview is because they lack the knowledge or skill to perform the job*

Not true! Employers are keen to point out that a lack of knowledge or skill often does lead to rejection. However, many times it's factors such as poor communication skills, failing to answer the questions, lack of preparation for the interview, lack of confidence and poor personal appearance which largely contribute to the decision to reject.

# REMEMBER

✔ Never jump into making an immediate career decision. Take time to analyse the job offer carefully.

✔ If the offer documentation you've received isn't clear, contact the personnel manager or recruitment consultant and ask for clarification.

✔ If, on balance, you believe the company's salary offer undervalues you, try a little negotiation to bring about an improvement.

✔ If, after careful consideration, you decide to decline the offer, send a suitably worded letter to the employer.

✔ If you've formally accepted an offer of employment and you're currently employed, you'll have to tender your resignation in writing.

✔ Leave your current employer on good terms and give them the full period of notice to which they're entitled.

✔ When you receive letters of rejection, don't dwell on this for too long; think of it as a learning experience.

✔ Don't ask for feedback from an interview: this is unpopular with most interviewers. Instead, send a short letter to thank the interviewer and ask to be considered for any similar future vacancies.

✔ The most positive way of dealing with rejection is to look again at your interview evaluation form, and take steps to improve your performance.

✔ It's important to remain positive and optimistic throughout the process of job search and interviews.

# part two  other selection methods

# Psychometric tests

## A TESTING TIME

Testing has been in use for more than 50 years; however, its use has grown significantly in recent years, and the signs are that as the selection process becomes more important in the changing world of work, tests are here to stay.

Tests are used for a number of purposes, including career counselling, team-building, assessment and development. However, for many organisations, the most common use of tests is in the recruitment and selection process.

Psychometric or psychological tests measure aptitude, ability, attainment or intelligence and individual differences in personality. They provide the recruiter with additional relevant information over and above that obtained from the selection interview. For instance, tests aid the recruitment process by ensuring that all candidates are treated fairly and measured against a common yardstick. Many recruiters also believe that selection tests enable a more objective analysis to take place than is possible when only using interviews. It is because tests are now seen as effective predictors of performance that they have seen a significant growth.

Tests are said to be reliable and valid. In test jargon, validity means that when compared with other selection methods, such as interviews, they're more likely to actually test what they claim to test. This means the test must be related to the demands of the job and be able to predict success or failure, otherwise it's of no use. Reliability means consistency of interpretation. The questions should be free of ambiguity so that whoever takes the test will interpret them in the same way. Similarly, irrespective of whether you take a test on a Monday in March or a Friday in June, you should score more or less the same.

Most tests are designed and developed by occupational psychologists, who also produce what is commonly known as normative data. This is the information that allows employers to compare the scores of tested candidates against the scores of a normal population of similar people. For example, if you happen to be a graduate, your score would be compared with those of other graduates.

There are numerous tests available to employers. Unfortunately, many are poorly constructed and don't really measure what they're supposed to do. However, there are also reputable test developers and publishers whose tests have been independently evaluated, such as Saville & Holdsworth Ltd (SHL) and Oxford Psychologists Press.

One concern shared by all reputable test developers and publishers is that those people who score and interpret test results should be trained to at least the standard approved by The British Psychological Society, an organisation concerned with testing standards and with systems for accrediting competence in test use.

Because it is recognised that interviews can be an imperfect selection tool, an increasing number of organisations are using tests to enhance the decision-making process for selection. If you're actively searching for your next job or a career change, it's highly probable that you will, at some point, be exposed to the world of psychometric tests. This chapter explains what you can expect if you're invited to sit a test. This is followed by descriptions of the most common tests and a number of practice questions.

## MYTH BUSTER

### *Psychometric tests are the same as academic tests*

Not true! Psychometric tests are not academic tests. Whilst some tests may resemble exams, they don't have the same aims. If, for example, you had recently taken the GCSE exam in maths, it wouldn't bother the maths examiner if your spelling was poor. However, any battery of psychometric tests is generally seeking a comprehensive picture of what you can and can't do.

## WHAT TO EXPECT ON THE DAY OF THE TEST

Most tests are conducted under 'examination' type conditions. This is to ensure, as far as possible, that all candidates are treated in the same manner. They usually take place before an interview and on separate days. This is to provide time for the tests to be scored.

When you receive your invitation to sit the test, this should, with any luck, include a leaflet explaining the purpose of the test with several sample questions. This will give you some idea of what to expect on the day of the test. Work through the practice questions and try to understand how the correct answers are reached for each question. Make a note of any points or questions you might want to ask at the test session.

The night before, make sure you get a good night's sleep so that you feel refreshed and alert the following morning. Set off in good time for the test venue. When you arrive, you'll be shown to a seat facing the test administrator and will be provided with all the necessary materials, such as pencils, erasers and possibly a small amount of blank paper.

The test administrator will hand out test booklets and separate answer sheets so that they can be scored quickly.

The purpose of the test and how it will be conducted will then be explained. Listen carefully to the instructions. For some tests, there is a strict time limit and the administrator will use a stopwatch to control this.

At the top of each answer sheet, you'll find space for your name, date of birth and the date of the test. Many tests also include some sample questions and an explanation of the test procedure. You'll be encouraged to ask the administrator for help if you're not sure about anything. Obviously, the administrator won't give you the answers to the questions, but they should point you in the right direction.

Once the test is over and the administrator has collected the test booklets and answer sheets, you'll be able to leave.

'I'd certainly recommend to anyone that they put in some practice if they expect to be sitting selection tests. Practice can result in significant improvements in performance in most ability tests. It also boosts confidence and helps people to cope with apprehension and anxiety.'

*Recruitment and development officer – clothing manufacturers*

'In my view, selection tests are a fair way of selecting staff as long as the process also includes interviews. The best employers are those who explain the purpose of the test and offer feedback to those who want it.'

*University graduate – Southeast*

## TESTS USED IN THE SELECTION PROCESS

A variety of tests are used in the selection process, but the two you're most likely to encounter are:

- ability tests
- personality questionnaires.

Practice material has been provided in this chapter, the answers to which can be found on page 93.

# ABILITY TESTS

These tests assess a selection of occupational abilities across a wide range of staff, from school-leavers to senior management, and are perhaps the most commonly used tests in the field of employment. They tend to fall into two groups: aptitude tests and attainment tests. Aptitude tests are used to predict the potential of a candidate for a particular job, whilst attainment tests measure abilities or skills already acquired by training or experience. Aptitude tests measure:

- verbal ability
- numerical ability
- clerical and computing skills
- spatial ability
- diagrammatic and mechanical reasoning
- manual dexterity.

Organisations using ability tests for selection purposes will probably have a clear understanding of the job and the type of work it involves. For example, when applying for the post of engineer, candidates might be asked to complete a test of mechanical ability, because this is likely to play an important part in the job.

For graduate positions, many companies use a broad battery of tests to get a feel for a person's abilities in different areas. This is likely to include tests of verbal ability, numerical reasoning, possibly abstract problem-solving and critical reasoning, in conjunction with personality questionnaires.

Ability tests employ multiple-choice questions conducted under exam conditions with strict time limits. The questions have definite right and wrong answers. If you're asked to sit an ability test, this will typically comprise two or three separate sections. Although there are many different types of ability tests, normally one section will contain questions that measure verbal ability, another numerical ability, and perhaps a third will measure spatial ability or diagrammatic reasoning.

### Some further tips

In addition to the advice given in the section 'What to expect on the day of the test', here are some further tips for sitting ability tests:

- At the start of the test, quickly work out how much time you have for each question. Put your watch in front of you and work with 'quiet urgency'. Keep an eye on the time as you work through the questions.
- Follow the instructions for providing your answer: this may involve placing a tick or cross in a box, filling in a box, circling or underlining the chosen answer.
- Don't spend too long on any one question. If you don't know the answer, then move on to the next question. Only when you've completed the test, and there's enough time left, should you go back to the unanswered questions.
- Resist the temptation to check each answer thoroughly until you're absolutely convinced it's right: you'll waste far too much time.
- Sometimes the questions get harder as you work through the test. Later questions might therefore take longer to answer than the earlier ones. So it's important not to fall behind the clock; time lost on the first few questions is almost impossible to make up.
- If calculators are allowed, use your own – you're familiar with how it works.
- Finally, try not to be panicked by the time pressure.

## PRACTICE QUESTIONS

### Verbal ability

These tests measure vocabulary, spelling and the grammatical skills essential in the drafting and processing of correspondence, along with the ability to understand written information. Their complexity varies depending on the nature of the job for which they're being used. For example, when used to select professional staff, these tests can measure the ability to interpret high-level written information and evaluate the logic of arguments.

Here are some practice examples of questions used in verbal ability tests. Answers can be found on page 93.

*1. Test of verbal interpretation for sales and customer service roles*[1]
This test consists of a passage of text followed by several statements. Your task is to evaluate each statement given the information or opinions contained in the passage, and to mark the appropriate circle in the answer section applying the following rules:

**Mark circle A**
**TRUE:** the statement is true given the information or opinions contained in the passage.

**Mark circle B**
**FALSE:** the statement is false given the information or opinions contained in the passage.

**Mark circle C**
You **CANNOT SAY** whether the statement is true or false without further information.

This is a timed test.

> The international travel business has been hard hit in recent years, a problem that has impacted severely on the hotel industry. Despite this, hotels are now fighting back by transferring attention from attracting tourists to attracting business travellers. One popular way of doing this is by creating an 'Executive Floor'. These floors are specially designed to provide business people with communal facilities such as personal computers, facsimile machines and photocopiers. Rooms on 'Executive Floors' are supplied with complimentary business magazines and newspapers, and more money is spent on decorating and furnishing these rooms than on other hotel rooms.

1. Rooms on 'Executive Floors' are decorated more economically than other parts of hotels.
2. More business travellers than ever before are now staying in hotels.
3. The hotel industry is now shifting its attention away from holiday-makers.
4. Guests staying on the 'Non-Executive Floors' do not get free newspapers.

## 1. Verbal interpretation answer section

1.    (A)    (B)    (C)

2.    (A)    (B)    (C)

3.    (A)    (B)    (C)

4.    (A)    (B)    (C)

*2. Test of verbal evaluation for supervisory and junior management roles*[2]

This test consists of a passage of text followed by several statements. Your task is to evaluate each statement given the information or opinions contained in the passage, and to colour in the appropriate circle in the answer section applying the following rules:

**Mark circle A**
**TRUE:** the statement is true given the information or opinions contained in the passage.

**Mark circle B**
**FALSE:** the statement is false given the information or opinions contained in the passage.

**Mark circle C**
You **CANNOT SAY** whether the statement is true or false without further information.

This is a timed test.

Many organisations find it beneficial to employ students during the summer. Permanent staff often wish to take their own holidays over this period. Furthermore, it is not uncommon for companies to experience peak workloads in the summer and so require extra staff. Summer employment also attracts students who may return as well-qualified recruits to an organisation when they have completed their education. Ensuring that the students learn as much as possible about the organisation encourages their interest in working on a permanent basis. Organisations pay students on a fixed rate without the usual entitlement to paid holidays or sick leave.

1. It is possible that permanent staff who are on holiday can have their work carried out by students.
2. Students in summer employment are given the same paid holiday benefit as permanent staff.
3. Students are subject to the organisation's standard disciplinary and grievance procedures.
4. Some companies have more to do in summer when students are available for vacation work.

## 2. Verbal evaluation answer section

1.  (A)    (B)    (C)

2.  (A)    (B)    (C)

3.  (A)    (B)    (C)

4.  (A)    (B)    (C)

*3. Test of verbal comprehension for skilled operatives and technical supervisors*[3]
For each question, choose the correct answer from the five possible answers. Choose the word which best completes the following sentence. Colour in the appropriate circle in the answer section. This is a timed test.

1. | All employees should [＿＿＿＿＿＿] from such a training scheme.

| A | B | C | D | E |
|---|---|---|---|---|
| result | credit | succeed | enrol | benefit |

2. | Hard is to soft as hot is to [＿＿＿＿＿＿]

| A | B | C | D | E |
|---|---|---|---|---|
| cool | warm | cold | icy | tepid |

3. | Which of the following words is closest to toxic?

| A | B | C | D | E |
|---|---|---|---|---|
| putrid | poisonous | bitter | contagious | inedible |

4. | All exposed pipes will have to be [＿＿＿＿＿＿] to protect them from freezing.

| A | B | C | D | E |
|---|---|---|---|---|
| insulated | regulated | connected | incorporated | hot |

5. | Which of the following words is closest to vertical?

| A | B | C | D | E |
|---|---|---|---|---|
| horizontal | parallel | straight | perpendicular | flat |

3. Verbal comprehension answer section

1. (A) (B) (C) (D) (E)

2. (A) (B) (C) (D) (E)

3. (A) (B) (C) (D) (E)

4. (A) (B) (C) (D) (E)

5. (A) (B) (C) (D) (E)

## Numerical ability

These tests aim to identify strengths in understanding and reasoning with numbers.

Here are some practice examples of questions used in numerical ability tests. Answers can be found on page 93.

*4. Test of numerical interpretation for sales and customer service roles*[1]

In this test you will be using facts and figures presented in the table to answer questions designed to assess your ability to reason with data. In each question you are given five answers to choose from. One, and only one, of the answers is correct in each case. You may use a calculator. Mark the appropriate circle in the answer section. This is a timed test.

| TELEPHONE CALLS RECEIVED BY CUSTOMER SERVICES THIS MONTH | | | | |
|---|---|---|---|---|
| Person taking call | No. of product enquiries | No. of complaints | No. of account queries | Total no. of calls |
| Jo | 155 | 6 | 6 | 167 |
| Mark | 310 | 2 | 10 | 322 |
| Michelle | 205 | 0 | 47 | 252 |
| Susan | 112 | 14 | 25 | 151 |
| Tony | 370 | 8 | 35 | 413 |

1. How many product enquiries were received this month?

| A | B | C | D | E |
|---|---|---|---|---|
| 1142 | 1152 | 1182 | 1232 | 1292 |

2. If each complaint call lasted for an average of 12 minutes, how much time was spent dealing with complaint calls?

| A | B | C | D | E |
|---|---|---|---|---|
| 5 hours 12 mins | 5 hours 24 mins | 5 hours 36 mins | 5 hours 48 mins | 6 hours |

3. Two-thirds of complaining customers received a £15 voucher and the rest received a £50 voucher. What was the total value of these vouchers?

| A | B | C | D | E |
|---|---|---|---|---|
| £500 | £760 | £800 | £1,010 | £1,150 |

**4. Numerical interpretation answer section**

1. Ⓐ   Ⓑ   Ⓒ   Ⓓ   Ⓔ

2. Ⓐ   Ⓑ   Ⓒ   Ⓓ   Ⓔ

3. Ⓐ   Ⓑ   Ⓒ   Ⓓ   Ⓔ

*5. Number series test for staff working in information technology*[4]
In the questions below, find the number which replaces the question mark in the series. Colour in the appropriate circle in the answer section. This is a timed test.

1. | 2 | ? | 8 | 16 |

| A | B | C | D | E |
|---|---|---|---|---|
| 3 | 4 | 5 | 6 | 7 |

2. | 15 | 13 | ? | 9 | 7 |

| A | B | C | D | E |
|---|---|---|---|---|
| 10 | 11 | 12 | 13 | 14 |

3.

| 1/3 | 2/6 | 3/9 | 4/12 | ? |

| A | B | C | D | E |
|---|---|---|---|---|
| 5/12 | 5/13 | 5/15 | 6/15 | 6/16 |

4.

| 1.5 | 3.0 | 4.5 | ? | 7.5 |

| A | B | C | D | E |
|---|---|---|---|---|
| 5 | 5.5 | 6 | 6.5 | 7 |

5.

| 3 | 4 | 6 | 7 | ? |

| A | B | C | D | E |
|---|---|---|---|---|
| 9 | 10 | 11 | 12 | 13 |

**5. Number series answer section**

1. (A)   (B)   (C)   (D)   (E)

2. (A)   (B)   (C)   (D)   (E)

3. (A)   (B)   (C)   (D)   (E)

4. (A)   (B)   (C)   (D)   (E)

5. (A)   (B)   (C)   (D)   (E)

*6. Test of numerical reasoning for managers and professional staff*[5]

Choose the correct answer from the five options given for each question. You may use a calculator. Colour in the appropriate circle in the answer section. This is a timed test.

| 1. | If a maintenance contract costs £87 per month and a technician call-out not under a maintenance contract £325, how many call-outs per year would make the contract worthwhile? |
|---|---|

| A | B | C | D | E |
|---|---|---|---|---|
| 4 | 5 | 6 | 7 | 8 |

| 2. | If every 250 bottles of bleach require 16.25 litres of solvent to produce, how much solvent is required to produce 6,500 bottles of bleach? |
|---|---|

| A | B | C | D | E |
|---|---|---|---|---|
| 42.3 litres | 100.0 litres | 121.9 litres | 422.5 litres | 1,219.0 litres |

| 3. | Last year's sales target was £265,000. This year's is £328,000. By what percentage has this year's target increased over last year's? |
|---|---|

| A | B | C | D | E |
|---|---|---|---|---|
| 17% | 29% | 43% | 81% | none of these |

| 4. | A total of 5,200 analyses last month required 17,300 hours of computer time. Approximately how much computer time would be required to perform an additional 300 analyses if all other factors remain unchanged? |
|---|---|

| A | B | C | D | E |
|---|---|---|---|---|
| 330 hours | 540 hours | 660 hours | 940 hours | 1,000 hours |

**6. Numerical reasoning answer section**

1. (A)    (B)    (C)    (D)    (E)

2. (A)    (B)    (C)    (D)    (E)

3. (A)    (B)    (C)    (D)    (E)

4. (A)    (B)    (C)    (D)    (E)

## Clerical and computing skills

As their names suggest, these tests deal with the skills needed to work in an automated office.

Here are some practice examples of questions used in tests of clerical and computing skills. Answers can be found on pages 93 to 96.

*7. Coded instructions test for school-leavers and work-experienced applicants[6]*

This test consists of a series of passages containing instructions, each of which is followed by a number of questions. You are to use the instructions in each passage to answer the questions which follow that passage. Colour in the appropriate circle in the answer section.

You are carrying out a computer check of personnel records.

> If the staff member has left the organisation, enter code L alone into the computer. For all staff members still present code P together with the appropriate code below.
>
> If the home address has changed, enter code A; otherwise enter code B. If the home telephone number has changed, enter code T. If the home telephone number is the same, enter code C.
>
> If the name of the staff member's doctor has changed, enter code D; otherwise enter code N. If the doctor's telephone number has changed, enter code R. If the telephone number is the same, enter code S.
>
> Code letters are to be entered in the sequence given above.

Which codes should be used to show the following records?

1. Employee number 1 is still a staff member. His address has changed but he has kept the same telephone number. There is no change to his doctor's details.

A   PANS
B   ACNS
C   PACNS
D   PANCS
E   PACSN

2.  Employee number 2 changed her doctor a year ago but in the past month has left the organisation.

A   LR
B   LNR
C   RL
D   L
E   LRN

3.  Employee number 3 is still a staff member. His address and telephone number are the same and so is the name of his doctor. However, his doctor is operating from a different address and telephone number.

A   PBCR
B   PBCRN
C   PCN
D   LPBCR
E   PBCNR

**7. Coded instructions answer section**

1. (A)    (B)    (C)    (D)    (E)

2. (A)    (B)    (C)    (D)    (E)

3. (A)    (B)    (C)    (D)    (E)

## Spatial ability

These tests measure the ability to recognise shapes and locate differences between shapes and designs. Here are some practice examples of questions used in spatial ability tests. Answers can be found on pages 93 to 96.

*8. Spatial reasoning test for staff working in information technology*[4]
In this test, you are given a pattern which, if cut out, could be folded to make a three-dimensional shape (a box). You must decide which, if any, of the four boxes

could be made by folding the pattern, and indicate this by colouring in the appropriate circle. If you think that none of the boxes could be made from the pattern, fill in circle 'E' in the answer section. This is a timed test.

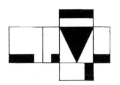

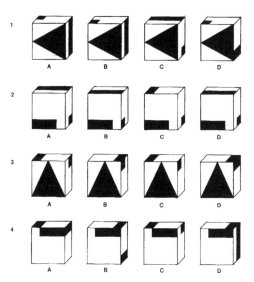

## 8. Spatial reasoning answer section

1. (A)    (B)    (C)    (D)    (E)

2. (A)    (B)    (C)    (D)    (E)

3. (A)    (B)    (C)    (D)    (E)

4. (A)    (B)    (C)    (D)    (E)

## Diagrammatic and mechanical reasoning

As their names suggest, these tests deal with diagrams and mechanical concepts. Here are some practice examples of questions used in diagrammatic reasoning and mechanical reasoning tests. Answers can be found on pages 93 to 96.

*9. Diagrammatic thinking test for technical-level apprenticeship schemes*[7]

In this test you are required to follow the progress of a 'Development figure', which is changed according to instructions contained in a series of 'Process boxes'. These boxes are divided into three levels, each of which affects the development figure in a given way.

| Process box | | |
|---|---|---|
| Level 1 | x | means change SHAPE from circle to square or vice versa |
| Level 2 | x | means change SIZE from large to small or vice versa |
| Level 3 | x | means change COLOUR from black to white or vice versa |

NB: The absence of a cross means no change to that aspect of the figure.

Your task is to identify which process needs to be repeated at the end of the series in order to achieve the required 'Target' figure. Indicate your answer by colouring in the appropriate circles A, B, C or D in the answer section.

Development figures                    Target figures

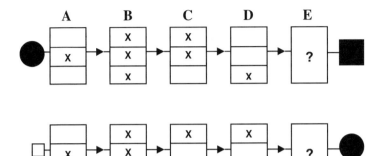

## 9. Diagrammatic thinking answer section

1.    (A)    (B)    (C)    (D)

2.    (A)    (B)    (C)    (D)

## Manual dexterity

These tests are not pencil and paper tests; they assess manual dexterity skills relevant to many assembly jobs in manufacturing and production industries.

# ANSWERS TO THE PRACTICE QUESTIONS

### Test 1

1. B

2. C

3. A

4. C

**Test 2**

1. ● B C
2. A ● C
3. A B ●
4. ● B C

**Test 3**

1. A B C D ●
2. A B ● D E
3. A ● C D E
4. ● B C D E
5. A B C ● E

**Test 4**

1. B

2. E

3. C

**Test 5**

1. A ● C D E
2. A ● C D E

3. (A)　(B)　●　(D)　(E)

4. (A)　(B)　●　(D)　(E)

5. ●　(B)　(C)　(D)　(E)

**Test 6**

1. ●　(B)　(C)　(D)　(E)

2. (A)　(B)　(C)　●　(E)

3. (A)　(B)　(C)　(D)　●

4. (A)　(B)　(C)　(D)　●

**Test 7**

1. (A)　(B)　●　(D)　(E)

2. (A)　(B)　(C)　●　(E)

3. (A)　(B)　(C)　(D)　●

**Test 8**

1. (A)　●　(C)　(D)　(E)

2. (A)　(B)　(C)　●　(E)

3. (A)　(B)　●　(D)　(E)

4. (A)　(B)　(C)　(D)　●

## Test 9

1. (A)    (B)    ●    (D)

2. ●    (B)    (C)    (D)

---

### Case Study
### Selection tests

Jane had been invited to sit a selection test by two employers, one of which was a local government department. On both occasions, the selection tests were tests of ability. Unfortunately, Jane failed both sets of tests.

Jane knew that she'd failed by only a few marks, so several months later she decided to ask for some advice on how to improve her performance. A friend and university lecturer suggested that she should spend a week practising maths and English exercises. Books containing these exercises were available on loan from her local careers service, and several others were found in the reference section of a large public library. Jane set aside two hours of practice every day for the next five days. On the last day, she practised answering the questions against the clock. 'I found working in the library the perfect setting, because it was so quiet and there were no distractions. After five days, my understanding of the questions had greatly improved and I felt much more confident.'

Later in the year, Jane was offered an opportunity to sit the selection tests again by the same local government department. On the day before the tests, she went back to the library to spend a few hours with the practice material. 'One week after sitting the tests, I received a letter to say I'd passed and was to be offered a post in the department.'

## PERSONALITY QUESTIONNAIRES

Personality questionnaires are designed to assess aspects of personality relevant to work, such as interpersonal relationships, work attitudes and values, flexibility and the way people approach their work. The use of these questionnaires in selection has increased in popularity in the wake of a growing body of evidence that strongly correlates personality traits with job performance.

The two most commonly used personality questionnaires are the Raymond Cattell's 16 Personality Factor Questionnaire (16PF) and the Occupational Personality Questionnaire (OPQ), devised by Saville & Holdsworth Ltd. These tests are concerned with the broad range of personality traits that are generally relevant to the world of work. The 16PF questionnaire measures 16 underlying personality characteristics that influence the way in which an individual behaves. The OPQ measures 30 dimensions of personality in three sectors: relationships with people, thinking style, and feeling and emotions.

In a personality questionnaire, you are likely to be asked how you'd behave in a variety of typical situations. For example, after reading a number of phrases or statements, you'd be asked to rate yourself, stating whether you agree with the statement, disagree with the statement or if your opinion falls in between. An example might be:

'I get slightly embarrassed if I suddenly become the focus of attention in a social group.'

a.   yes
b.   in between
c.   no.

You could also be asked to choose from a number of statements, indicating which you think is least true or typical of you. Clearly, there are no right or wrong answers to these questions, only your personal profile.

These tests often contain hundreds of questions and, although not timed, can take anywhere from 30 to

90 minutes to complete. The tester enters all the test scores on to a profile and weighs them statistically to compare them with the scores of a normal population of similar people. From this, it is possible to predict the candidate's future behaviour in a new job.

## MYTH BUSTER

### *Personality questionnaires are really personality tests*

*Not true! It is misleading to talk about personality questionnaires as tests, because this implies there's a pass or fail score, which isn't the case.*

### A question of feedback

Anyone sitting a personality questionnaire needs to know that feedback will be available to them at some stage. Normally, this is forthcoming at the end of the selection process. Professionally provided, feedback can be invaluable to candidates actively job seeking or changing their career. If the employer doesn't refer to feedback arrangements during the introduction to the questionnaire, feel free to raise the matter. Once you've left the employer's premises, it may be too late to do anything about it.

> 'After sitting several different personality questionnaires, I found the feedback really helpful and constructive. I disagreed with one or two comments, but the process enabled me to question some of the assumptions I'd made about myself.'
>
> University graduate – Northwest

### Some tips

- If the instructions for completing the questionnaire are unclear, ask the administrator for guidance.

- Follow the instructions for providing your answers; this may involve placing a tick or cross in a box, filling in a box, circling or underlining the chosen answer.
- Although there's no time limit, you should work quickly rather than pondering at length over any one question. A person's first or gut response is the best indication of how they'd generally respond in the situation.
- Make sure you answer all the questions.
- Don't try to give the answers you think the recruiter wants. Many questionnaires contain questions which help to check if someone is describing themselves honestly and consistently, so try to be as accurate as possible when answering the questions.
- Ask about feedback. Psychologists are ethically bound to make feedback available to people undergoing assessment. Remember, it could prove useful both in the job, if you're successful, or in future job applications.

## PRACTICE QUESTIONS

Here are some practice examples of questions used in personality questionnaires.[8]

### Making choices

In this example you are given a block of four statements: A, B, C and D. Your task is to choose the statement which you think is most true or typical of you in your everyday behaviour, and then choose the one which is least true or typical of you. Indicate your choices by filling in the appropriate circle in the row marked 'M' (for Most) and in the next row 'L' (for Least).

The first block has been completed for you. The person has chosen 'Enjoys organising people' as most true (or typical) and 'Seeks variety' as being least true (or typical) of him/her. Now try questions 2, 3 and 4 yourself.

I am the sort of person who …

1.  A  Has a wide circle of
       friends                    Ⓜ Ⓐ ● Ⓒ Ⓓ
    B  Enjoys organising
       people
    C  Relaxes easily            Ⓛ Ⓐ Ⓑ Ⓒ ●
    D  Seeks variety

2.  A  Helps people with
       their problems            Ⓜ Ⓐ Ⓑ Ⓒ Ⓓ
    B  Develops new
       approaches
    C  Has lots of energy        Ⓛ Ⓐ Ⓑ Ⓒ Ⓓ
    D  Enjoys social activities

3.  A  Has lots of new ideas     Ⓜ Ⓐ Ⓑ Ⓒ Ⓓ
    B  Feels calm
    C  Likes to understand
       things                    Ⓛ Ⓐ Ⓑ Ⓒ Ⓓ
    D  Is easy to get on with

4.  A  Enjoys organising events  Ⓜ Ⓐ Ⓑ Ⓒ Ⓓ
    B  Sometimes gets angry
    C  Is talkative              Ⓛ Ⓐ Ⓑ Ⓒ Ⓓ
    D  Resolves conflicts at work

*References*

1.  *Customer Contact Test, practice leaflet* © SHL Group plc
    1996.
2.  *Critical Reasoning Test, practice leaflet* © SHL Group plc
    1991.
3.  *Technical Test Battery, practice leaflet* © SHL Group plc
    1992.
4.  *Information Technology Test Series, practice leaflet* © SHL
    Group plc 1992.
5.  *Advanced Managerial Tests, practice leaflet* © SHL Group
    plc 1993.

6. *Automated Office Battery, practice leaflet* © SHL Group plc 1986.
7. *Applied Technology Tests, practice leaflet* © SHL Group plc.
8. *An Introduction to Personality Questionnaires* © SHL Group plc 1996.

## REMEMBER

✔ Psychometric tests measure aptitude, ability, attainment or intelligence and individual differences in personality.

✔ Employers compare the scores of tested candidates against the scores of a normal population of similar people.

✔ If you're actively searching for your next job or a career change, it's highly probable that you will, at some point, be exposed to the world of psychometric tests.

✔ Most tests are conducted under 'examination' type conditions.

✔ The tests you're most likely to encounter are ability tests and personality questionnaires.

✔ Ability tests assess a range of occupational abilities. They employ multiple-choice questions that have definite right and wrong answers.

✔ Prepare for ability tests by reading the relevant section in this chapter and completing the practice questions.

✔ Personality questionnaires are designed to test aspects of personality relevant to work.

✔ The two most commonly used personality questionnaires you're likely to encounter are the 16PF and OPQ.

✔ Anyone sitting a personality questionnaire needs to know that feedback will be available to them at some stage.

## WHAT IS AN ASSESSMENT CENTRE?

The term 'assessment centre' does not refer to a location, but to a process which is being increasingly used by middle to large organisations in the UK to assess the most suitable candidates for a wide range of jobs and to identify staff who possess strong potential for promotion.

Assessment centres offer a multiple assessment approach to the selection process. They don't aim to test specific knowledge and technical skills. Rather, they attempt to simulate the actual job and then endeavour to achieve a precise fit between the test environment and the work environment. Then, with the aid of a set of varied exercises that are designed to reproduce different aspects of the work environment, participants are given an opportunity to display their skills and competencies. These exercises may last anywhere from half a day to two days, and are usually conducted away from the employer's workplace.

Whilst the process is intensive and fairly stressful, it also provides additional opportunities for those who feel that they're unable to demonstrate their abilities as strongly during the interview. Assessment centres give participants a practical working idea of what the employer expects from their staff, and also provide opportunities to network with other candidates.

Assessment centres involve a lot of time and expense, so many employers will only use them after the initial stages of the selection process, when, for instance, a shortlist has been drawn up. Other measures, such as psychometric tests, may complement the selection process.

## MYTH BUSTER

### *Assessment centres are only used for the selection of graduates during the milk round*

Not true! Whilst the use of assessment centres for graduate recruitment is popular amongst large employers in the private sector, these same employers are increasing their use of assessment centres for recruiting managers and specialists. In addition, the public sector uses assessment centres primarily for general external recruitment.

## HOW ASSESSMENT CENTRES ARE CONDUCTED

Assessment centres are highly structured in their design, application and assessment procedure. In some cases, they are conducted by trained human resources staff from within the company; in other instances by outside consultants. The structure and content of each assessment centre can vary depending on the industry and the job in question. For example, in business, the exercises would probably include leadership, problem-solving and negotiation; whereas for jobs in the communications industry, there might be a greater emphasis on creative ideas and prose style.

The focus of the centre is on behaviour, and exercises are used to capture and simulate the key areas of the job. Performance is measured in terms of the competencies required to achieve the target level of performance in a particular job. Here are some examples of the competencies used in assessment centres:

- written communication
- oral communication
- intellectual skills

- organising and planning skills
- problem-solving
- decision-making
- skills of persuasiveness
- motivation
- creativity
- analytical and reasoning skills.

At the beginning of the assessment centre, participants are given a briefing about the timetable of exercises and the location of rooms. Before each exercise, an assessor describes what is involved, the participant's role and the timescale.

During each exercise, a group of trained assessors rates individual candidates against the indicators included in that exercise using a prescribed performance scale. The exercises are designed to draw out from participants those behaviours that are regarded as important to the successful performance of a particular job. Results are then cross-compared against the same indicators measured in other tests. Following completion of the assessment centre, assessors discuss the test results and reach a group consensus about each participant's rating.

## MYTH BUSTER

### Candidates are assessed on the quantity of their input

Not true! This is a common misunderstanding amongst those who attend assessment centres. Exercises may well be structured to measure people management, teamwork, negotiation and problem-solving skills. However, domineering behaviour doesn't equate to leadership skills.

# THE MOST COMMON TYPES OF EXERCISES

The most common types of exercises include:

- group exercises
- individual exercises
- in-tray exercises
- role-plays
- presentations.

There are no rules on how many exercises should be included in an assessment centre, except that they must cover all aspects of the required competence. Several psychometric tests may also be included, such as ability tests and personality questionnaires.

## Group exercises

Group exercises involve participants working together as a team to resolve a presented issue. In these exercises, assessors are looking for behavioural evidence of:

- participation and contribution
- analysis and presentation of a reasoned argument
- communication
- listening abilities
- negotiation and co-operation.

Discussion groups may range from:

- 'leaderless ones', where everyone has the same brief and works towards the objective of achieving some sort of consensus decision
- the 'assigned role', where each person has a different brief so that they go into the meeting with a hidden agenda
- discussions where each participant is asked to take the chair.

More often than not with these exercises, it's not the solution itself but how it was arrived at that's important: how you got on with the other members of the group, whether you listened to their contributions, etc.

## Individual exercises

Individual exercises can range from writing an essay on a given topic to undertaking a project. You will be given a generous amount of factual information, which is generally ambiguous, and, in some cases, contradictory. You will then be expected to communicate your findings in the form of a written report or presentation to the assessors. It's important that the assessors know how you arrived at your decision and that this is clearly articulated.

## In-tray exercises

With in-tray exercises you will assume a particular role as an employee of a fictitious company and then deal with the problems contained in a sample pile of letters, memos, reports, faxes, phone messages and e-mails. The sample will vary in importance, urgency and complexity. You'll probably be asked to respond to each sample in writing and keep a record of your 'reasons for action' to discuss with an assessor. In a typical exercise you might, for example, be a supervisor who at short notice has had to step into their manager's shoes. A crisis is developing, which you're expected to resolve. Meanwhile, you must continue to deal with the other items in your in-tray. Mail is also delivered and collected every half-hour.

In-tray exercises measure your organising, prioritising, analytical and problem-solving skills as well as written communication abilities.

## Role-plays

In role-playing exercises you'll once again assume a fictitious role and deal with an irate customer or handle a grievance. This type of exercise may measure oral communication, customer service orientation and problem-solving.

## Presentations

Increasingly, employers are looking for people who have good communication skills. Often during an assessment centre, you'll be asked to give a short presentation on a given topic. You may get advance notice of this, but take note, you could be thrown in at the deep end. In other instances, armed with a particular problem and some background information, you'll be asked to demonstrate how you'd go about finding a solution to the problem.

## THE IMPORTANCE OF FEEDBACK

As a participant in an assessment centre, you can expect to be given feedback. If the assessors don't mention this before you leave the employer's premises, then make a point of asking about it. If you haven't been selected, then you'll naturally be disappointed. However, you should still find the process of feedback constructive, because it will concentrate on your development needs.

'If you've been asked to attend an assessment centre, it's worth knowing that there's a large body of academic research which suggests that the assessment centre is probably one of the most valid predictors of performance in a job. If correctly structured, it's probably one of the fairest and most objective means of gathering information upon which to base a selection decision.'
*Senior lecturer, management studies – college of further education*

'Keep in mind that all assessment centres aren't the same; you may meet some exercises at one centre but not at another. After the assessment centre has finished, most applicants usually find the experience to be enjoyable and they often learn a lot about themselves, even if they didn't think so at the time.'
*Assessment centre leading assessor*

## HOW TO PREPARE FOR AN ASSESSMENT CENTRE

Here are a few ideas to help you prepare for the assessment centre:

- You cannot study for an assessment centre, but it may help if you have some idea of what to expect. If you've had some previous experience with ability tests and personality questionnaires, this will certainly be an advantage. Most important of all, adopting a positive mental attitude towards the process will prove invaluable.

- If you've been given some reading material beforehand, make sure you read this carefully and understand what's required of you.

- Re-familiarise yourself with the job description and any useful information about the employing organisation. You might find some clues as to the type of employee they're seeking.

- The night before the test, make sure you get a good night's sleep so that you feel refreshed and alert the following morning.

- Talk to friends who've attended assessment centres and ask for their views and opinions. Find out how they coped with the process.

- Be yourself – bring your own personality and experience to the assessment centre. Aim to act as naturally as possible.

- If you think you've performed badly in one particular exercise, don't let this affect your performance on other exercises.

- Don't guess what's being measured – this may affect your performance and assessment.

- View the assessment centre as an opportunity to learn about the employer and the position for which you've applied.

- Consider the process as a positive learning experience.

## Case Study
## Assessment centres

Victoria was in the final year of her degree course in English literature when the annual milk round recruitment exercise began in November. After attending a number of presentations, Victoria expressed an interest in a company recruiting management trainees. She completed and returned their application form.

During December, Victoria received an invitation from the company to attend an interview at the university. The interview went well and Victoria received a further invitation to attend a two-day assessment centre at a hotel in Oxford. The invitation contained helpful information, including the types of activities that would be included.

'All eight candidates arrived early evening and met up in the hotel bar, where we were introduced to the assessors. The following morning we were formally welcomed to the centre, and the leading assessor explained that the centre provided a multiple assessment approach to the selection of candidates. Four assessors would observe and document the performance of the candidates during a series of exercises, which had been specially designed to draw out those behaviours considered to be important in successfully performing a management role in the company.'

The first event was a battery of ability tests and personality questionnaires followed by a second interview. 'This was a much more detailed interview, where we were presented with a range of hypothetical situations to resolve. Later in the afternoon, we were all presented with an in-tray exercise. We were each given an in-tray containing a range of documents that you'd expect to find in a manager's in-tray after they returned to work from a week's holiday. We were given one hour to answer all the letters and memos.'

The second day began with a group exercise. 'We were each given the same work-related problem to solve, but each person had different information in their brief. The objective was to talk the problem through as a team, discuss the pros and cons of each person's suggested answer to the problem, and present a single agreed solution to the leading assessor. The assessors observed the entire process.'

For the last exercise, each candidate was asked to assume the fictitious role of Customer Service Manager. 'I was asked to deal with a number of customer complaints, both face to face and on the phone. The whole process was videotaped and played back to us at the end of the exercise.'

At the conclusion of the assessment centre, each candidate was given feedback from one of the assessors. 'I enjoyed the experience of the assessment centre much more than I anticipated,' said Victoria, 'and the feedback was particularly helpful and constructive.'

# REMEMBER

✔ Assessment centres offer a multiple assessment approach to the selection process.

✔ Assessment centres attempt to simulate the actual job and then endeavour to achieve a precise fit between the test environment and the work environment.

✔ The structure and content of each assessment centre can vary depending on the industry and the job in question.

✔ The focus of the centre is on behaviour, and exercises are used to capture and simulate the key areas of the job.

✔ The exercises are designed to draw out from participants those behaviours that are regarded as important to the successful performance of a particular job.

✔ The most common types of exercises include group exercises, individual exercises, in-tray exercises, role-plays and presentations.

✔ During each exercise, a group of trained assessors rate individual candidates.

✔ Several psychometric tests may be included as part of the assessment centre.

✔ The process of feedback is constructive, because it will concentrate on your development needs.

✔ Consider the process as a positive learning experience.

## GRAPHOLOGY

### Origins and history

Handwriting analysis is by no means a recent development. Its origins are said to stem from ancient Greece and Rome. However, serious research only started during the 19th century, when a group of French monks began a study of hundreds of different samples of handwriting. The monk in charge of this study, Abbé Jean Hippolyte Michon, founded the Society of Graphology in Paris and later became known as the grandfather of graphology. In 1871, he invented the word 'graphology' from two Greek words: *graph*, meaning 'writing', and *-ology*, a suffix that denotes scientific study. Michon produced rules for interpreting handwriting based on the 'fixed-sign' theory, where one graphic sign indicated one specific personality trait. A primitive and superficial method of analysing handwriting, this would no longer be acceptable as the sole means of interpretation today.

Jules Crépieux-Jamin, a pupil of Michon, developed the system further. Adopting a holistic approach, he was more interested in studying the overall pattern of the handwriting.

The French continued to dominate the field of graphology until the end of the 19th century, when a German university professor, Wilhelm Preyer, originated the idea that handwriting is essentially 'brain writing'. Germany produced several more important contributors to graphology, whilst developments also took place in Belgium, Hungary, the Netherlands, England and America. In 1929 in the US, a man named Milton Bunker founded the standardised system of graphology known as Graphoanalysis, which is still in use today.

Today, the status of graphology reflects its somewhat chequered past, as competing theories vie with each other. In America, whilst handwriting analysis has gained some ground, it still has a long way to go before it reaches the level of acceptance it enjoys in countries such as France, Germany and Switzerland.

## Graphology as a method of selection

Handwriting analysis as a selection tool is widely used in parts of mainland Europe, especially Spain, Switzerland and France. It undoubtedly enjoys broad acceptance amongst the French business community, where up to 75% of French companies are said to use graphology as an aid to staff selection. Employers make a point of asking job applicants to supply a handwritten letter of application and CV. Thankfully, French personnel executives don't rely on handwriting alone, but use it as an additional device in conjunction with interviews and other tests to improve selection decisions.

In the UK, acceptance of graphology has been slow to spread. A survey of 500 companies conducted by the Institute of Personnel and Development during 1996 suggested that 9% of small companies (those with fewer than 100 people) were using handwriting analysis. This compared with 1% of medium-sized companies (100–499 staff) and 5% of large companies (500 plus staff). However, because of the European market, it does seem that more UK companies will come under pressure from their continental partners to provide graphological profiles of management candidates, while European companies will probably wish to introduce their standard selection procedures into their UK subsidiaries.

## How does it work?

When we first learn to write, we conform to a specific style, referred to by graphologists as 'copybook'. Gradually, as we develop, we begin to deviate in varying degrees from copybook and evolve a style that's uniquely our own. The extent of this variation is taken by graphologists as a measure of the writer's individuality, maturity, originality, intelligence, ethical standards and general lifestyle. All these aspects of the writer's personality are then deduced from a careful study of the principal handwriting features – size, slant, speed, pressure, layout, forms of connection, broadness or narrowness, etc.

Certain kinds of information, however, can't be gleaned from a handwriting sample, such as age, sex and whether the person is left- or right-handed. As age and sex have a bearing on the character analysis, these facts have to be established at the start.

'People often don't want to give too many clues about themselves, but with graphology you have the whole person laid out on paper.'

*Graphology expert*

'I am of the opinion that the preponderance of scientific evidence is just too negative for employers to use graphology as an aid to the selection process. Until there's substantial, scientifically sound evidence presented, I believe that graphology should be written off.'

*HR director – building industry*

'I have a suspicion that the real attraction of graphology for some employers is that it can be used without the subject's knowledge, which is a practice I strongly disapprove of.'

*Headhunter*

## JOB SIMULATIONS

Job simulations involve the design and administration of tests that closely match the tasks involved in the jobs for which selection is taking place. The common sense basis for this approach is that the best way of discovering how well a person is likely to do a job is to give them the job to do. Of course, it's not possible within any normal selection process to produce a simulation that fully replicates the actual employment experience. Anything from a week to several months of actual working is needed to provide a full assessment of a person's capabilities in every aspect of the job, whereas simulations have to select key elements of the job for testing and compress the process into a feasible time-frame. Despite such limitations, well-designed tests of this kind can offer reliable predictions.

To design a job simulation, the employer must first analyse the job by identifying its central tasks and the skills and other qualities that are required to perform them to an acceptable standard. However, sometimes these may not be the elements that lend themselves most readily to simulation. In this case, other selection methods such as psychometric tests may be included to address these factors.

Most employers agree that job simulation isn't a perfect selection method. However closely the actual work can be replicated, the context, and probably the timescales, won't match reality. For this reason, job simulation tends to be used as one element of the selection process, with interviews and psychometric tests now being built in.

## ASTROLOGY

Those who believe in astrology are convinced that the stars and planets influence our every action. For many, the only contact with astrology is limited to the entertainment value of horoscopes in the daily newspapers.

The use of astrology in selection is rare; and those who do use it usually do so secretly. To prepare an astrological assessment, an astrologer must know the candidate's time, place and date of birth to determine the relative positions of the planets, sun and moon. Astrology claims to predict the candidate's future and their ability to do the job. It also uses the candidate's personal details to determine whether they're likely to be compatible with other people in the company.

It's highly unlikely that you'd know if astrology was being used as part of the selection process; and since you can't do anything to prepare for it, it's best to take a philosophical view and acquiesce.

## PSYCHIC METHODS

Even more controversial than astrology are the psychic methods adopted by a handful of recruiters. Psychics can be called on to sit in on job interviews and give an opinion on the candidates. They claim to be able to see the candidate's aura, or electromagnetic field, which shows how a person is feeling or lacking emotionally.

Understandably, recruiters keep quiet about using psychic methods. If you suspected that this method was being used in your interview, it would probably be best to give that particular employer a wide berth.

---

### REMEMBER

✔ Handwriting analysis is by no means a recent development. Its origins are said to stem from ancient Greece and Rome. However, serious research only started during the 19th century.

✔ Handwriting analysis as a selection tool is widely used in parts of mainland Europe, especially Spain, Switzerland and France.

✔ In the UK, acceptance of graphology has been slow to spread.

✔ It seems that more UK companies will come under pressure from their European partners to provide graphological profiles of management candidates.

✔ Aspects of a writer's personality are obtained by a careful study of the principal handwriting features – size, slant, speed, pressure, layout, forms of connection, broadness or narrowness, etc.

✔ Job simulations involve the design and administration of tests that closely match the tasks involved in the jobs for which selection is taking place.

✔ Job simulation has tended to become merely one element of the selection process, with interviews and psychometric tests now being built in.

✔ The use of astrology in selection is rare.

✔ Because astrology is based on a study of the relative positions of the planets, sun and moon at the time and date of your birth, you can do nothing to prepare for this fringe method of selection.

✔ If you suspect that psychic methods are being used in your case, consider carefully whether you want to work for an employer who uses such controversial techniques.

## 10 Conclusion

Perhaps the single most important piece of advice you could find in this book would be *businesslike presentation*. Putting in the time and effort to prepare for interviews and other selection methods is a vital part of your strategy to win your next job. Consider also the following important features:

- Learn all you can about the employers and the jobs for which you've applied.
- Practise your answers to interview questions and prepare some questions of your own.
- Dress professionally and take pride in your appearance when attending interviews.
- Be aware at all times of the importance of body language. Your confidence will receive a welcome boost, and feeling good about yourself will raise your self-esteem.
- Put on your best performance on the day of the interview.
- Evaluate your performance after the interview has ended.

If you combine all these features with the knowledge, guidance, hints and encouragement contained in these pages, you should have no difficulty putting together your own strategy for dealing with interviews and other selection methods; but the effort must come from you and must be sustained.

Successful people usually display a tenacious determination to achieve their goal. They also have the capacity for hard work. If you're equal to your preferred job, and combine this same philosophy with your new-found strategy for dealing with interviews and other selection methods, then you have an excellent chance of succeeding.

In this guide you will find a list of transferable skills and a personal strengths and weaknesses inventory. When ranking your transferable skills **1** is your strongest asset.

## LIST OF TRANSFERABLE SKILLS

| People skills | Tick this box ✔ if this skill applies to you | Tick this box ✔ if this skill needs further development | Rank each of your skills |
|---|---|---|---|
| Advising – *Recommending a course of action.* | | | |
| Caring – *Having a strong feeling or concern for others.* | | | |
| Coaching – *Guiding the activities of others.* | | | |
| Communicating – *Conveying, receiving and sharing information.* | | | |
| Contacting – *Keeping in touch.* | | | |
| Counselling – *Helping people with personal, emotional and work problems.* | | | |
| Delegating – *Handing over tasks to subordinates. Briefing them correctly and monitoring their performance.* | | | |
| Encouraging – *Inspiring someone with confidence.* | | | |
| Handling complaints – *Dealing with grievances, justified and unjustified, from staff and members of the public.* | | | |
| Influencing – *Persuading someone to alter or agree with a particular course of action.* | | | |
| Instructing – *Teaching. Making known to someone what you require him or her to do.* | | | |

| | Tick this box ✔ if this skill applies to you | Tick this box ✔ if this skill needs further development | Rank each of your skills |
|---|---|---|---|
| **People skills** *continued* | | | |
| Interviewing – *Assessing someone's suitability for a job. Obtaining information using a questioning technique.* | | | |
| Leading – *Encouraging and inspiring individuals and teams to give their best to achieve a desired result.* | | | |
| Listening – *Gathering information whilst establishing rapport with the speaker.* | | | |
| Managing – *Deciding what to do and then getting it done through the effective use of people and other resources.* | | | |
| Mediating – *Bringing about a settlement, agreement or compromise between two or more parties. Acting as a liaison between competing interests.* | | | |
| Negotiating – *Setting objectives, deciding on strategy, and persuading and bargaining to get agreement and commitment.* | | | |
| Organising – *Getting things done in a well-ordered, efficient and methodical manner.* | | | |
| Selling – *Persuading someone to buy a product or service.* | | | |
| Speaking in public – *Communicating with an audience to motivate, inform or entertain.* | | | |
| Supervising – *Overseeing and inspecting work or workers.* | | | |
| Training – *Bringing a person or group of people to an agreed standard of proficiency by practice and instruction.* | | | |

| Reasoning and judging skills | Tick this box ✔ if this skill applies to you | Tick this box ✔ if this skill needs further development | Rank each of your skills |
|---|---|---|---|
| Analysing – *Examining in detail to break down into components or essential features.* | | | |
| Appraising – *Evaluating programmes or services, judging the value of something, evaluating the performance of people.* | | | |
| Calculating – *Performing mathematical computations, assessing the risks of an activity.* | | | |
| Decision-making – *Choosing between priorities and options.* | | | |
| Designing – *Inventing, describing and depicting the parts or details of something according to a plan.* | | | |
| Editing – *Checking and improving the accuracy of documents.* | | | |
| Evaluating – *Judging or assessing the value of something.* | | | |
| Generating alternatives – *Producing a choice between two or more items or courses of action.* | | | |
| Innovating – *Creating and developing new ideas or solutions to problems.* | | | |
| Interpreting data – *Explaining or clarifying the meaning of facts or figures.* | | | |
| Investigating – *Analysing, evaluating and seeking new solutions.* | | | |
| Problem-solving – *Using reason to reach solutions.* | | | |
| Reviewing – *Examining to determine whether changes should be made.* | | | |
| Shaping – *Planning and moulding something into a desired form.* | | | |
| Validating – *Assuring the certainty of something in order to dispel any doubt.* | | | |

| Co-ordinating skills | Tick this box ✔ if this skill applies to you | Tick this box ✔ if this skill needs further development | Rank each of your skills |
|---|---|---|---|
| Administering – *Taking charge of an area of work or tasks.* | | | |
| Arranging – *Making preparations and plans.* | | | |
| Assembling – *Gathering together a collection of parts.* | | | |
| Constructing – *Building or erecting together parts as a whole.* | | | |
| Controlling – *Comparing what's being achieved with what should have been achieved and, when appropriate, taking corrective action.* | | | |
| Co-ordinating – *Blending things together to achieve a desired result.* | | | |
| Developing – *Expanding or improving to an enhanced state.* | | | |
| Driving – *Operating and guiding a motor vehicle.* | | | |
| Erecting – *Raising or constructing (a building, for example).* | | | |
| Fitting – *Installing, connecting or attaching.* | | | |
| Identifying priorities – *Establishing the best order.* | | | |
| Inspecting – *Examining carefully and critically for flaws.* | | | |
| Liaising – *Contacting and communicating on a regular basis.* | | | |
| Mechanical dexterity – *Able to work with machinery.* | | | |
| Monitoring – *Observing and checking.* | | | |
| Operating equipment – *Being in charge of a working piece of equipment.* | | | |
| Optimising – *Making the most effective use of something.* | | | |
| Planning – *Formulating a programme for the achievement of an objective.* | | | |
| Predicting – *Forecasting outcomes.* | | | |
| Timing – *Organising time efficiently so that tasks are completed in a set period.* | | | |
| Trouble-shooting – *Locating and eliminating sources of trouble.* | | | |

| Information skills | Tick this box ✔ if this skill applies to you | Tick this box ✔ if this skill needs further development | Rank each of your skills |
|---|---|---|---|
| Budgeting – *Outlining the cost of a project; assuring that spend will not exceed available funds; using money efficiently.* | | | |
| Classifying – *Arranging or organising according to class or category.* | | | |
| Clerical – *Describing skills used by those working in offices.* | | | |
| Compiling – *Gathering numerical, statistical data, accumulating facts about a given topic.* | | | |
| Computing – *Describing skills used by operators of high-tech equipment.* | | | |
| Corresponding with – *Communicating by letter.* | | | |
| Data-gathering – *Collecting information for analysis.* | | | |
| Diagnosing – *Investigating and determining the nature of a problem.* | | | |
| Dispensing information – *Giving out information in various formats.* | | | |
| Drafting reports – *Preparing provisional documents, the content of which are subject to approval before being released.* | | | |
| Fact-finding – *Discovering accurate information.* | | | |
| Information extraction – *Drawing out information.* | | | |
| Numerical – *Working effectively with numbers.* | | | |
| Observing – *Watching carefully.* | | | |
| Recording – *Keeping an account of events or facts to serve as a source of information for the future.* | | | |
| Researching – *Investigating or enquiring in order to gather information about a subject. Physical observations.* | | | |
| Surveying – *Inspecting or examining in a comprehensive and detailed way the condition or quantity of a given subject.* | | | |

| **Information skills** *continued* | Tick this box ✔ if this skill applies to you | Tick this box ✔ if this skill needs further development | Rank each of your skills |
|---|---|---|---|
| Updating – *Keeping a file of information up to date. Completing records or acquiring new information on an old topic.* | | | |
| Writing – *Communicating using the written word.* | | | |

| **Originating skills** | Tick this box ✔ if this skill applies to you | Tick this box ✔ if this skill needs further development | Rank each of your skills |
|---|---|---|---|
| Achieving – *Successfully accomplishing something because of effort, skill or perseverance.* | | | |
| Anticipating – *Staying one step ahead. Being able to sense changes. Expecting it before it happens.* | | | |
| Creating – *Producing new ideas, plans and new ways of looking at things.* | | | |
| Establishing – *Creating and setting up something.* | | | |
| Initiating – *Beginning or introducing something.* | | | |
| Promoting – *Raising awareness in others of a subject's benefits.* | | | |
| Responsibility-taking – *Willingly taking control of something.* | | | |
| Visualising – *Being able to picture things in the mind.* | | | |

| Personal strengths | Achievement rating | | |
|---|---|---|---|
| | **Small** | **Moderate** | **Significant** |
| Able to maintain confidentiality | | | |
| Able to take risks | | | |
| Able to work under stress | | | |
| Accurate | | | |
| Adaptable | | | |
| Ambitious | | | |
| Assertive | | | |
| Caring | | | |
| Confident | | | |
| Conscientious | | | |
| Courageous | | | |
| Creative | | | |
| Decisive | | | |
| Dependable | | | |
| Diligent | | | |
| Diplomatic | | | |
| Enthusiastic | | | |
| Even-tempered | | | |
| Flexible | | | |
| Genuine | | | |
| Good under pressure | | | |
| Helpful | | | |

| Personal strengths | Achievement rating | | |
|---|---|---|---|
| | Small | Moderate | Significant |
| Honest | | | |
| Imaginative | | | |
| Independent-minded | | | |
| Intuitive | | | |
| Inventive | | | |
| Loyal | | | |
| Organised | | | |
| Original | | | |
| Outgoing | | | |
| Patient | | | |
| Perceptive | | | |
| Persistent | | | |
| Positive | | | |
| Practical | | | |
| Punctual | | | |
| Quick-thinking | | | |
| Rational | | | |
| Reliable | | | |
| Resilient | | | |
| Resourceful | | | |
| Responsible | | | |
| Self-disciplined | | | |

| Personal strengths | Achievement rating | | |
|---|---|---|---|
| | **Small** | **Moderate** | **Significant** |
| Self-reliant | | | |
| Self-starting | | | |
| Shows initiative | | | |
| Sociable | | | |
| Spontaneous | | | |
| Strong work ethic | | | |
| Systematic | | | |
| Tactful | | | |
| Tenacious | | | |
| Thorough | | | |
| Thoughtful | | | |
| Tidy | | | |
| Tolerant | | | |
| Trustworthy | | | |
| Truthful | | | |
| Understanding | | | |
| Versatile | | | |
| **Weaknesses** | | | |
| Avoids confrontation | | | |
| Dogmatic | | | |
| Domineering | | | |
| Emotional | | | |

| Personal weaknesses | Achievement rating | | |
|---|---|---|---|
| | **Small** | **Moderate** | **Significant** |
| Forthright | | | |
| Headstrong | | | |
| Impractical | | | |
| Impulsive | | | |
| Inconsiderate | | | |
| Inconsistent | | | |
| Indecisive | | | |
| Laid back | | | |
| Meddlesome | | | |
| Naïve | | | |
| Obsessive | | | |
| Obstinate | | | |
| Over-cautious | | | |
| Perfectionist | | | |
| Quarrelsome | | | |
| Reckless | | | |
| Self-opinionated | | | |
| Single minded | | | |
| Too demanding of others | | | |
| Uninspiring | | | |
| Workaholic | | | |

## INTERNET RECRUITMENT

### Search engines

**www.excite.com**
**www.excite.co.uk**
**www.infoseek.com**
**www.lycos.com**
**www.lycos.co.uk**
**www.webcrawler.com**
**www.yahoo.com**
**www.yahoo.co.uk**
**www.god.co.uk**
**www.ukplus.co.uk**

### UK online recruitment websites

The Appointments Section – Offers a range of IT and telecommunications jobs.
Contact: **www.taps.com**

Job Hunter – Updated daily by the UK's regional press.
Contact: **www.jobhunter.co.uk**

Jobmail – Offers jobs in IT, education, engineering and the legal sector.
Contact: **www.jobmail.co.uk**

Jobs Go Public – Specialises in jobs in the public sector, charity and voluntary sectors.
Contact: **www.jobsgopublic.com**

Jobs in Food – Offers all types of jobs in catering.
Contact: **www.cateringnet.co.uk**

Jobs in UK Journalism – Specialises in vacancies for journalists looking for work in magazines and newspapers in the UK and worldwide.
Contact: **www.journalism.co.uk**

Jobserve – Claims to be the largest source of IT vacancies in the UK.
Contact: **www.jobserve.com/**

Jobsite – Offers a range of vacancies.
Contact: **www.jobsite.co.uk**

The Language Site – Offers jobs for specialists in translation work.
Contact: **www.interscript.com/**

Marketing Week – Offers marketing jobs and articles appearing in the magazine.
Contact: **www.marketingweek.co.uk/index.htm/**

The Monster Board – Offers a range of jobs.
Contact: **www.monster.co.uk**

Netjobs – Offers a range of vacancies.
Contact: **www.netjobs.co.uk**

Personnel Health – Specialises in healthcare jobs.
Contact: **www.personnelnet.com/**

Prospects website – Association of Graduate Careers Advisory Services (AGCAS). For jobs and occupational information.
Contact: **www.prospects.csu.man.ac.uk**

Jobsunlimited – *The Guardian*'s site.
Contact: **www.jobsunlimited.co.uk**

Top Jobs on the Net – Offers a range of general positions.
Contact: **www.topjobs.net**


## NEWSPAPERS

| National newspaper job advertisements | | |
| --- | --- | --- |
| **Newspaper** | **Day of the week** | **Job sector** |
| *Daily Mail* | Tuesday | Clerical |
| | | Secretarial |
| | Thursday | Clerical |
| | | Engineering |
| | | General Appointments |
| | | Overseas |
| | | Printing & Publishing |
| | | Retail |
| | | Sales |
| | | Technical |
| *Daily Telegraph* | Thursday | Executive/Management |
| | | General Appointments |
| *The European* | Wednesday | General Appointments in the European Community |
| *The Express* | Thursday | Catering/Hotel |
| | | Engineering |
| | | General Appointments |
| | | Sales |
| | | Technical |
| *Financial Times* | Wednesday | Banking |
| | | Finance |
| | | General Appointments |
| | Thursday | Accountancy |
| | | Finance |
| *The Guardian* | Monday | Creative & Media |
| | | Fund-raising |
| | | Marketing |
| | | PR |
| | | Sales |
| | | Secretarial |

| National newspaper job advertisements | | |
|---|---|---|
| **Newspaper** | **Day of the week** | **Job sector** |
| The Guardian | Tuesday | Education<br>General Appointments |
| | Wednesday | Environment<br>Health<br>Housing<br>Public Sector |
| | Saturday | Careers<br>Creative & Media<br>Education<br>General Appointments<br>Graduates<br>IT<br>Marketing<br>PR |
| The Independent | Tuesday<br>Wednesday | Public Sector<br>Sales<br>Science<br>IT<br>Accounting<br>Banking<br>Clerical |
| | Thursday | Finance<br>Legal |
| The Independent on Sunday | Sunday | Office |
| Mail on Sunday | Sunday | Multilingual |
| The Observer | Sunday | Secretarial<br>Education<br>Graduates<br>General Appointments<br>All Sectors<br>IT |
| Scotsman | Monday<br>Tuesday<br>Wednesday | General Appointments<br>General Appointments<br>General Appointments<br>Education |
| | Thursday | General Appointments<br>Public Sector |
| | Friday | General Appointments<br>Marketing<br>Sales |

| National newspaper job advertisements | | |
|---|---|---|
| **Newspaper** | **Day of the week** | **Job sector** |
| Sunday Telegraph | Sunday | Repeat of Thursday's Appointments Supplement |
| The Sunday Times | Sunday | All Sectors |
| The Times | Wednesday | Secretarial |
| | Thursday | Management Senior Appointments Secretarial |
| | Friday | Education Marketing Media Sales |

## A SELECTION OF OTHER PUBLICATIONS CARRYING JOB ADVERTISEMENTS

| | |
|---|---|
| Accountancy Age | Weekly |
| Architects' Journal | Weekly |
| Artists and Illustrators | Monthly |
| Banker, The | Monthly |
| British Journal of Photography | Weekly |
| British Medical Journal | Weekly |
| Building | Weekly |
| Caterer & Hotelkeeper | Weekly |
| Chemist & Druggist | Weekly |
| Community Care | Weekly |
| Education | Weekly |
| Engineering | Monthly |
| Farmers' Weekly | Weekly |
| Financial Advisor | Weekly |

| | |
|---|---|
| *Grocer, The* | Weekly |
| *Housebuilder* | Monthly |
| *Insurance Age* | Monthly |
| *Lawyer, The* | Weekly |
| *Local Government Chronicle* | Weekly |
| *Marketing Week* | Weekly |
| *Media Week* | Weekly |
| *Money Marketing* | Weekly |
| *New Civil Engineer* | Weekly |
| *New Media Age* | Weekly |
| *Nursing Times & Nursing Mirror* | Weekly |
| *People Management* | Bi-monthly |
| *Printing World* | Weekly |
| *Retail Weekly* | Weekly |
| *Soap Perfumery & Cosmetics* | Monthly |
| *Sports Trader* | Monthly |
| *Surveyor* | Weekly |
| *Travel Trade Gazette* | Weekly |
| *Woodworker, The* | Monthly |

## NETWORKING FOR WOMEN WEBSITE ADDRESSES

Women into Business (part of the Small Business Bureau). Contact: **www.smallbusinessbureau.org.uk/women/index.htm**

Network for Successful UK Women. Contact: **www.networkwomenuk.org/**

# USEFUL ADDRESSES

## Sources of career and industry information

Many of these organisations can provide you with useful career information or background to their industry. Send a letter setting out the information you require and for what purpose.

### Administrative and clerical

Association of Medical Secretaries, Practice Administrators and Receptionists Ltd
Tavistock House North
Tavistock Square
London WC1H 9LN
Tel: 020 7387 6005

### Advertising

The Advertising Association
Abford House
15 Wilton Road
London SW1V 1NJ
Tel: 020 7828 2771

### Ambulance services

London Ambulance Service
The Recruitment Department
Central Division HQ
St Andrews House
St Andrews Way
Devons Road
London E3 3PA
Tel: 020 7887 6638

### Animals

Animal Care College
Ascot House
29a High Street
Ascot
Berkshire SL5 7JG
Tel: 01344 628269

British Veterinary Nursing Association Ltd
Level 15
Terminus House
Terminus Street
Harlow
Essex CM20 1XA
Tel: 01279 450567

RSPCA
The Causeway
Horsham
West Sussex RH12 1HG
Tel: 0990 555999

## Architecture
Architects and Surveying Institute
15 St Mary Street
Chippenham
Wiltshire SN15 3WD
Tel: 01249 444505

## Art and design
Association of Illustrators
81 Leonard Street
London EC2A 4QS
Tel: 020 7613 4328

Chartered Society of Designers
1st Floor
32–38 Saffron Hill
London EC1N 8SG
Tel: 020 7831 9777

## Banking
Chartered Institute of Bankers
4–9 Burgate Lane
Canterbury
Kent CT1 2XJ
Tel: 01227 762600

**Beauty and hairdressing**
Hairdressing and Beauty Industry Authority
Fraser House
Netherhall Road
Doncaster DN1 2PH
Tel: 01302 380000

National Hairdressers' Federation
11 Goldington Road
Bedford MK40 3JY
Tel: 01234 360332

**Civil service**
The Establishment Officer
Ordnance Survey
Romsey Road
Maybush
Southampton SO16 4GU
Tel: 02380 792000

**Communications**
Federation of Communications Services
Keswick House
207 Anerley Road
London SE20 8ER
Tel: 020 8778 5656

**Computing**
National Training Organisation for Information Technology
16–18 Berners Street
London W1P 3DD
Tel: 020 7580 6677

**Construction**
Construction Industry Training Board
Newton Training Centre
Bircham Newton
King's Lynn
Norfolk PE31 6RH
Tel: 01485 577577

### Dentistry
British Dental Association
64 Wimpole Street
London W1M 8AL
Tel: 020 7935 0875


British Association of Dental Nurses
11 Pharos Street
Fleetwood
Lancashire FY7 6BG
Tel: 01253 778631


### Engineering
Engineering Construction Industry Training Board
Blue Court
Church Lane
Kings Langley
Hertfordshire WD4 8JP
Tel: 01923 260000


The Engineering Careers Information Service
Enta House
14 Upton Road
Watford WD1 7EP
Tel: 0800 282167


### Environment
Environment Agency
Public Enquiries Department
Rio House
Waterside Drive
Aztec West
Almondsbury
Bristol BS32 4UD
Tel: 01454 624400

English Nature
Enquiry Service
Room 1E
Northminster House
Peterborough PE1 1UA
Tel: 01733 455100

**Finance**
The Institute of Financial Accountants
Burford House
44 London Road
Sevenoaks
Kent TN13 1AS
Tel: 01732 458080

Chartered Institute of Management Accountants
63 Portland Place
London W1N 4AB
Tel: 020 7637 2311

**Food and drink**
Food and Drink National Training Organisation
Training Executive
6 Catherine Street
London WC2B 5JJ
Tel: 020 7836 2460

**Gardening**
Royal Horticultural Society
Supervisor of Studies and Training
Wisley
Woking
Surrey GU23 6QB
Tel: 01483 224234

The Institute of Horticulture
14–15 Belgrave Square
London SW1X 8PS
Tel: 020 7245 6943

**Health service**
NHS Careers
PO Box 376
Bristol BS99 3EY
Tel: 0845 6060655

**Hotel and catering**
Hotel, Catering and International Management Association
191 Trinity Road
London SW17 7HN
Tel: 020 8672 4251

**Human resources and personnel**
Institute of Personnel and Development
Camp Road
Wimbledon
London SW19 4UX
Tel: 020 8971 9000

**Insurance**
The Chartered Insurance Institute
20 Aldermanbury
London EC2V 7HY
Tel: 020 7417 4793

**Languages**
The Institute of Linguists
Saxon House
48 Southwark Street
London SE1 1UN
Tel: 020 7940 3100

**Law**
The Law Society
Legal Education Information Unit
Ipsley Court
Berrington Close
Redditch
Worcestershire B98 0TD
Tel: 01527 517141

Crown Prosecution Service
Recruitment Branch
50 Ludgate Hill
London EC4M 7EX
Tel: 020 7796 8000

Institute of Legal Executives
Kempston Manor
Kempston
Bedfordshire MK42 7AB
Tel: 01234 841000

**Library work**
The Library Association
7 Ridgmount Street
London WC1E 7AE
Tel: 020 7255 0500

**Management**
Institute of Management
Management House
Cottingham Road
Corby
Northants NN17 1TT
Tel: 01536 204222

**Marketing**
The Chartered Institute of Marketing
Moor Hall
Cookham
Maidenhead
Berkshire SL6 9QH
Tel: 01628 427310

**Market research**
The Market Research Society
15 Northburgh Street
London EC1V 0JR
Tel: 020 7490 4911

## The media
National Council for the Training of Journalists
The Latton Bush Centre
Southern Way
Harlow
Essex CM18 7BL
Tel: 01279 430009

## Medical and nursing
British Medical Association
BMA House
Tavistock Square
London WC1H 9JP
Tel: 020 7387 4499

Royal College of Nursing
20 Cavendish Square
London W1M 0AB
Tel: 020 7409 3333

## Pharmacy
The Royal Pharmaceutical Society of Great Britain
1 Lambeth High Street
London SE1 7JN
Tel: 020 7735 9141

## Photography
Association of Photographers
31 Leonard Street
London EC2A 4QS
Tel: 020 7739 6669

## Physiotherapy
The Chartered Society of Physiotherapy
14 Bedford Row
London WC1R 4ED
Tel: 020 7306 6666

**Publishing and bookselling**
The Publishers Association
1 Kingsway
London WC2B 6X0
Tel: 020 7565 7474

Booksellers Association of Great Britain
272 Vauxhall Bridge Road
London SW1V 1BA
Tel: 020 7834 5477

**Sport**
Sport England
16 Upper Woburn Place
London WC1H 0QP
Tel: 020 7273 1500

Sports Council for Northern Ireland
House of Sport
Upper Malone Road
Belfast BT9 5LA
Tel: 02890 381222

Sport Scotland
Caledonia House
South Gyle
Edinburgh EH12 9DQ
Tel: 0131 317 7200

The Sports Council for Wales
Sophia Gardens
Cardiff CF11 9SW
Tel: 029 2030 0500

**Teaching**
Teaching Training Agency
Portland House
Stag Place
London SW1E 5TT
Tel: 020 7925 3700

## Travel and tourism
Institute of Travel and Tourism
113 Victoria Street
St Albans
Hertfordshire AL1 3TJ
Tel: 01727 854395

## Interim management
Albemarle Interim Management Services
26–28 Great Portland Street
London W1N 5AD
Tel: 020 7631 1991

Ernst & Young Corporate Resources
Roll House
7 Rolls Buildings
Fetter Lane
London EC4A 1NH
Tel: 020 7951 2000

Executive Interim Management
39 St James' Street
London SW1A 1JD
Tel: 020 7290 1430

PA Consulting Group
123 Buckingham Palace Road
London SW1W 9SR
Tel: 020 7730 9000

Russam GMS Ltd
48 High Street North
Dunstable
Bedfordshire LU6 1LA
Tel: 01582 666970

## Training and education

Information and advice can be obtained from the following:

Career Development Loans
Freepost
PO Box 354
Warrington WA4 6XU
Tel: 0800 585505

ECCTIS 2000
Oriel House
Oriel Road
Cheltenham
Gloucestershire GL50 1XP
Tel: 01242 252627

The Industrial Society
Robert Hyde House
48 Bryanston Square
London W1H 2EA
Tel: 020 7479 2000

Institute of Management
Management House
Cottingham Road
Corby
Northants NN17 1TT
Tel: 01536 204222

Institute of Personnel and Development
35 Camp Road
Wimbledon
London SW19 4UX
Tel: 020 8971 9000

Local Education Authorities (look in your local *Yellow Pages*)

National Extension College
18 Brooklands Avenue
Cambridge
CB2 2HN
Tel: 01223 450200

Open University
Admissions Office
PO Box 46
Milton Keynes MK7 6AP
Tel: 01908 274066

Royal Society of Arts
6 John Adam Street
London WC2N 6EZ
Tel: 020 7930 5115

## FURTHER READING

### Headhunters and recruitment consultants

*The Executive Grapevine*, published by Executive Grapevine International.

*CEPEC Recruitment Guide*, published by CEPEC Ltd.

*The Personnel Manager's Yearbook*, published by A. P. Information Services.

*Yearbook of Recruitment and Employment Services*, published by A. P. Information Services.

## Public speaking

Suzy Siddon, *Presentation Skills*, Institute of Personnel and Development, September 1999.

Rosemary Riley, *A Straightforward Guide to Public Speaking*, Straightforward Publications, July 1997.

Christina Stuart, *Be an Effective Speaker*, National Textbook Company, January 1999.

Roger Mason, *Teach Yourself Speaking at Special Occasions*, Teach Yourself Books, November 1995.

John Bowden, *Making Effective Speeches*, How To Books, October 1998.


# CAREER PUBLICATIONS FROM THE INDUSTRIAL SOCIETY

## The Insider Guides

### Job Search
Brian Sutton
ISBN 1 85835 815 9

### Career Networking
Brian Sutton
ISBN 1 85835 825 6

### Interviews & Assessments
Brian Sutton
ISBN 1 85835 820 5

## The Insider Career Guides

**Advertising, Marketing & PR**
Karen Holmes
ISBN 1 85835 872 8

**Banking & the City**
Karen Holmes
ISBN 1 85835 583 4

**Broadcasting & the Media**
Paul Redstone
ISBN 1 85835 867 1

**The Environment**
Melanie Allen
ISBN 1 85835 588 5

**Information & Communications Technology**
Jacquetta Megarry
ISBN 1 85835 593 1

**Retailing**
Liz Edwards
ISBN 1 85835 578 8

**Sport**
Robin Hardwick
ISBN 1 85835 573 7

**Travel & Tourism**
Karen France
ISBN 1 85835 598 2